ᒐ·ᑲᐸᔅ

Châhkâpâs

A Naskapi Legend

FIRST NATIONS LANGUAGE READERS
NASKAPI

ᒐ·ᑲᐸᐢ

Châhkâpâs

A Naskapi Legend

As told by
Elder John Peastitute

Edited and annotated
by Marguerite
MacKenzie

English literary
translation by
Julie Brittain

Illustrated by
Elizabeth Jancewicz

Project facilitation
and background notes
by Bill Jancewicz

FIRST NATIONS UNIVERSITY OF CANADA
SIFC

University of Regina Press

Cover and text design: Duncan Campbell, University of Regina Press

Cover art: "Woodland Caribou in Winter" by Mircea Costina / AdobeStock.

Illustrations in this volume are by Elizabeth Jancewicz.

Library and Archives Canada Cataloguing in Publication

TITLE: Châhkâpâs : a Naskapi legend / as told by Elder John Peastitute ; edited and annotated by Marguerite MacKenzie ; English literary translation by Julie Brittain ; illustrated by Elizabeth Jancewicz ; project facilitation and background notes by Bill Jancewicz.

NAMES: Peastitute, John, 1896-1981, author. | MacKenzie, Marguerite, editor. | Brittain, Julie, 1959- translator. | Jancewicz, Elizabeth, illustrator. | Jancewicz, Bill, 1955- writer of supplementary textual content. | Container of (work): Peastitute, John, 1896-1981. Châhkâpâs. | Container of (expression): Peastitute, John, 1896-1981. Châhkâpâs. English.

SERIES: First Nations language readers ; 7.

DESCRIPTION: Series statement: First Nations language readers ; 7 | Syllabics in title could not be transcribed. | Includes bibliographical references. | Text in Naskapi syllabics, Naskapi roman orthography, and in English translation.

IDENTIFIERS: Canadiana (print) 20210303883 | Canadiana (ebook) 20210307269 | ISBN 9780889778290 (softcover) | ISBN 9780889778313 (EPUB) | ISBN 9780889778306 (PDF)

SUBJECTS: LCSH: Legends—Naskapi Nation of Kawawachikamach. | LCSH: Naskapi Nation of Kawawachikamach. | LCSH: Naskapi language—Texts. | CSH: First Nations—Québec (Province)—Social life and customs. | LCGFT: Legends.

CLASSIFICATION: LCC E99.N18 P4313 2021 | DDC 398.2089/9732—dc23

10 9 8 7 6 5 4 3 2 1

U OF R PRESS

University of Regina Press, University of Regina
Regina, Saskatchewan, Canada, S4S 0A2
tel: (306) 585-4758 fax: (306) 585-4699
web: www.uofrpress.ca

We acknowledge the support of the Canada Council for the Arts for our publishing program. We acknowledge the financial support of the Government of Canada. / Nous reconnaissons l'appui financier du gouvernement du Canada. This publication was made possible through Creative Saskatchewan's Creative Industries Production Grant Program.

Canada Council for the Arts Conseil des Arts du Canada Canada creative SASKATCHEWAN

CONTENTS

ᒐ·ᑲᐸᔅ

Châhkâpâs / A Naskapi Legend

Foreword

It is a pleasure and a privilege to be able to present this collection of Naskapi *Châhkâpâs* stories as the seventh volume in our First Nations Language Reader (FNLR) series. Acknowledgement is gratefully extended to the Naskapi Development Corporation (NDC), the Naskapi people, and to all whose contributions made both its original publication (as part of the NDC's wonderful series of Naskapi Legends and Stories) and this volume possible. In particular, our gratitude is extended to the late John Peastitute for sharing his traditions with us all, and to Bill Jancewicz for facilitating the republication of these texts.

As part of the FNLR series, the current stories are firmly anchored in much that has preceded them. Most volumes thus far have come from the oral traditions of members of the Algonquian language family, and the Naskapi language of Labrador and Quebec is (along with Innu) among the easternmost of the Cree-Innu-Naskapi language continuum of that same Algonquian family. Still, this marks a significant expansion of our series in two ways. First, we are able to present the cycle of *Châhkâpâs* stories so important, in one form or another, to many of the Algonquian Peoples within Canada (see also the discussion in this book's Introduction). And this volume also provides our easternmost contribution thus far, such that we have now been able to highlight stories spanning nearly the entire geographic width of the north of Turtle Island, from the Lillooet in interior British Columbia to the Naskapi in Labrador. Future volumes promise only to continue to expand the variety of Indigenous languages and traditions that we are privileged to share.

For now, please enjoy the richness of these traditional Naskapi stories as presented by a consummate storyteller.

Arok Wolvengrey
âsimwâkw-pîsim, 2021

Introduction[1]

For centuries, the ancestors of the present-day Naskapi people lived and travelled across the subarctic tundra and taiga of the Ungava Peninsula in what is now northern Quebec and Labrador. They lived on the land, subsisting on the resources that could be found there. What made them unique among many other First Nations groups was their particular dependence upon the migratory caribou for sustenance and their nomadic lifestyle that stemmed from this dependence.

Like other Indigenous Peoples, the Naskapi have a long tradition of storytelling, passing histories and legends from generation to generation. And, like other Algonquian-speaking groups, the Naskapi distinguish two main genres of storytelling: *tipâchimûn* refers to an adventure or history in which the narrator himself or other eyewitnesses are characters in the story, while *âtiyûhkin* generally refers to a story which is from a distant "time before now," and often includes animal characters.

1 This introductory material has been modified from the original Naskapi Development Corporation (NDC) publication to align more consistently with University of Regina Press's First Nation Language Reader series publication guidelines.

It may be simple to say that the difference is merely that *tipâchimûna* (plural of *tipâchimûn*) are historical accounts while *âtiyûhkinch* (plural of *âtiyûhkin*) are myths or legends (Ellis 1988). But in truth, the dichotomy goes much deeper than this. *Tipâchimûna* may and often do contain fantastic, amazing, or unbelievable accounts—but *âtiyûhkinch* follow a strict and ancient narrative formula. Savard (1974) calls them "that which must be conveyed." In his treatise on the Wolverine stories, he says that the storyteller he worked with would never have considered the idea that someone could invent a new *âtiyûhkin*. These stories can only be transmitted from one storyteller to another.

John Peastitute

John Peastitute (1896–1981) was a Naskapi Elder who was well respected not only as a story-keeper, but also as a storyteller. His repertoire of both *tipâchimûna* and *âtiyûhkinch* was extensive, and his performances engaging. The tapes of his stories that have survived to be processed and studied are a precious legacy.

Marc Hammond, a compiler of Naskapi history, shared with us this summary of John's life (Hammond 2013, personal communication):

> John Peastitute, who died at Matimekosh in 1981, was born at the confluence of the Caniapiscau and Larch Rivers in 1896. He was one of nine children sired by *Sha-ba-deesh* (recorded as Jean Baptiste Katsas in the Hudson's Bay Company journals and regarded there as loyal to Révillon Frères as if to spite Hudson's Bay Company trader Peter McKenzie, his own father). *Sha-ba-deesh* died around 1919.
>
> John's own mother (*Sha-ee-at* to family and friends) hailed from a family who knew best the area northeast of Fort McKenzie (as far as the broad George River valley's lower reaches) and his "other" mother hailed

from a family whose members were and remained affiliated with Great Whale River.

While he knew best the area north and northwest of Fort McKenzie, where he hunted most of his adult life, John travelled during his lifetime virtually everywhere in traditional Naskapi territory (and then some), deferring to others who best knew the way and what was likely to be found. Before settling at Schefferville, John had gone even beyond traditional Naskapi territory as far as Sept-Îles (*Uashat*), North West River (*Sheshatshiu*), Davis Inlet (*Utshimassits*), and Great Whale River (*Whapmagoostui*) where some of his relatives would take their trade and eventually settle.

During the early 1920s, John married Susie Annie (1898–1988). They had nine children: John, Philip, Pete, Sam, Samson, Christina, Donald, Ruby, and Mannie: but only four (Philip, Christina, Donald, and Ruby) would live to see Schefferville.[2]

Apart from being a wide-ranging and, ordinarily, proficient hunter, John was a craftsman (as his son Philip would become). Although he never built a canoe of birch bark (as had his father), John was indeed one of the few men of his time who built canoes at all. He built canvas-covered ones, and this was only one of a number of traditions that John saw gradually disappear during his lifetime.

Stories about Chahkapas

The Chahkapas legend cycle is not uniquely Naskapi. This book contains a Naskapi representation of a body of "heroic" legends that are found in several other cultures across North America. There have been dozens of documented versions of these stories told in other language communities in the Algonquian language family. The earliest version was recorded in 1637 by

2 See the historical summary under the heading The Naskapi People, later in this introduction.

Father Paul Le Jeune in *The Jesuit Relations,* chapter x, and can be found in Volume XII of Thwaites's translation[3] of the *Relations* (Thwaites 1896–1901). Father Le Jeune wintered with a group of Innu (Montagnais) in 1633–1634, during which time he began to learn their language. Father Le Jeune's account of the *Tchakabech*[4] story, told to him by an Innu storyteller, is remarkable in its similarity to John Peastitute's version, even though it had been told nearly four centuries earlier.

Henry Rowe Schoolcraft, geographer and ethnologist during the first half of the 1800s, collected many North American legends and stories. He presents a version of "The Boy Who Set a Snare for the Sun," originally told in Ojibwe, in *Oneóta* (Schoolcraft 1845, p. 75). Schoolcraft was married to Jane Johnson, whose mother, an Ojibwe Chief's daughter, was married to a fur trader. Jane Johnson was a fluent speaker of Ojibwe and English, and had an extensive knowledge of Ojibwe legends. Her version of the Chahkapas story was collected near Sault Ste. Marie, Michigan, in the 1820s, 200 years ago and more than 1,500 kilometres away from where Father Le Jeune had collected the Innu version.

Another Ojibwe version of "ChakaPesh and the Moon Legend" (Morris 1989) was told by an Elder at Kitchenuhmaykoosib Inninuwug First Nation (Big Trout Lake), Ontario, and presented in two Ojibwe dialects in syllabics in the journal *Canadian Woman Studies.* This story was collected more than 2,000

3 For a more contemporary translation of the story collected by Father Le Jeune in *The Jesuit Relations*, see Randall (2011).

4 There are dozens of spellings of the protagonist's name *Chahkapas* throughout historical literature. An inexhaustive list was found on the Native Languages website (http://www.native-languages.org/tshakapesh.htm), as follows: *Chakapesh, Chakapish, Chikapash, Chaakaapaas, Tcikapis, Shikabish, Tsukabec, Tshakabesh, Djakabish, Tsuabec, Tcakabec, Tchakabech, Tcakapas, Tsja'bec, Tcika'pis, Cha-ka-bes, Sheecabish, Tcikabis, Chikabis, Tcikapec, Tcakabesh, Tcakapas, Tchakabech, Chahkabesh, Cahkapes, Cahkâpêsh, Jakabich, Chaakapesh, Tcakabish.*

kilometres away from the location where the Naskapi and Innu versions were collected.

American historian Francis Parkman recognized that such similarities between versions of tales told in different First Nations languages and communities indicated not only their wide diffusion but also provided evidence that these tales are immeasurably ancient (Parkman 1871, p. 38). Indeed today, thanks to the Internet, one can find several other renderings of the Chahkapas episodes told in related languages by contemporary storytellers, including versions in Atikamekw,[5] Innu,[6] and Cree. An extensive set of Cree stories with audio recordings were collected by C. Douglas Ellis, professor emeritus of linguistics at McGill University, Montreal, and currently adjunct research professor in the School of Linguistics and Applied Language Studies at Carleton University, Ottawa.

Ellis's 1995 book, *Âtalôhkâna Nêsta Tipâcimôwina: Cree Legends and Narratives from the West Coast of James Bay*, analyzes the theme, motifs, and character development of legends like *Chahkabesh* (Scott and Ellis 1995, pp. xxv–xxxv). In particular, he writes:

> A brief review of three of the tales of Chahkabesh provides further interesting examples of a carefully crafted

5 An Atikamekw version, "When Tcikabis Trapped the Sun," told by Anne Bouchard, was found at http://www.native-languages.org/atikstory.htm (retrieved March 2021).

6 One Innu version, "Tale of Tshakapesh," narrated by Charles Api Bellefleur, was found on the Nametau Innu website, along with an audio recorded version: http://www.nametauinnu.ca/en/culture/spirituality/tshakapesh (retrieved March 2021). Another Innu version found archived at the Native Languages website (temporarily relocated from the Innu Nation website, which at press time did not contain the stories) was "Tshakapesh and the Elephant Monster," told by Joseph Rich and Davis Inlet, and translated by Matthew Rich: http://www.bigorrin.org/archive109.htm (retrieved March 2021). A published version of this translation can be found in Peter Desbarats's book *What They Used to Tell about: Indian Legends from Labrador* (Desbarats 1969).

> frame which allows nonetheless for individual improvisation in developing the theme. Chahkabesh himself was a little fellow, represented by one storyteller as about six inches tall. Like Tom Thumb he compensated by ingenuity for the disadvantages attendant on his miniscule size. His curiosity about the world around him knew no bounds (Scott and Ellis 1995, p. xxvii).

Madeleine Lefebvre also gives a description and analysis of the exploits of *Tshakapesh*, suggesting that his special powers are connected with a mission to protect people from their enemies (such as *Kachituskw* and *Achaniskwaw*), and that his abilities related to his supernatural growth are related to being able to control the passage of time (Lefebvre 1974, p. 18). Rémi Savard likewise provides an exhaustive literary analysis of the structural motifs and variants of the *Tshakapesh* stories in his book, *La Voix des Autres* (Savard 1985). Savard's research project, which focused on collecting traditional Innu stories, played an important part in preserving this Naskapi version of Chahkapas as well. See the sections Recording the Stories and From Tape to Book in this introduction for more information.

Readers who are interested in digging deeper and learning more about the literary structure and discourse features of this kind of storytelling, along with other complete Swampy Cree versions of the Chahkapas story, are encouraged to read Ellis's book.[7] His presentation (and for readers of French, Lefebvre's and Savard's works as well) provides far more background and detailed analysis of the stories from a linguistic, literary, and cultural perspective. The present Naskapi volume and series is primarily focused on the goal of providing entertaining and readable Naskapi literature for Naskapi and English speakers.

This book presents the seven episodes of the Naskapi Chahkapas cycle in the same order that John Peastitute told the stories when his performance was recorded (see the section Recording the Stories in this introduction). Other traditions present

7 An online presentation of Ellis's collected recordings was found at the following website: http://www.spokencree.org/ (retrieved March 2021).

the episodes in a different order, and sometimes episodes are combined. For example, some elements of "Chahkapas and the Swing People" are found in the Swampy Cree (Winisk) episode "Chahkabesh and the Giant Women," and a single episode from that same collection (Scott and Ellis 1995)—"Chahkabesh Reaches for the Giant Beaver"—is performed here in two discontinuous episodes, "Chahkapas and the Bad People" (episode 4) and "Chahkapas's Sister Is Taken" (episode 6). In his analysis Savard (1985) charts all of the episodic variations.

Another significant source of variation is the identity of the monster Kachituskw referred to in the opening episode that tells the origin of Chahkapas. Several traditions describe the creature as a "stiff-legged bear,"[8] while Louis Bird (2007) says that Chahkapas's parents were killed by a giant cannibal, called *Achan*[9] in the Naskapi tradition. In the version of *Tchakabech* recorded by Le Jeune (Thwaites 1896–1901), a bear devours Chahkapas's father, but a great hare, *Michtabouchiou* (Innu *Mistapush*), devours his mother.

William Duncan Strong (1934), who wrote about the Chahkapas (*Djikábish*) story suggests that the monster in question was mammoth-like and says that his Naskapi informants were unanimous in describing the monster (*Kátcheetohúskw*) as having features like an elephant. However, Strong's contemporaries (Speck 1935, Michelson 1936, and Seibert 1937) were quick to refute Strong's conclusion, saying that the evidence that the creature was bear-like was much stronger. Lankford (1980) examines the question from a folklorist's point of view and also comes to the conclusion that the monster in the story must be bear-like, possibly even the "Ancient of Bears,"

8 In *Giving Voice to Bear*, David Rockwell writes, "The Stiff-legged Bear tale was common to the entire eastern sub-arctic. But the distribution of closely related tales, tales considered to be part of the same legend complex, is much larger . . . Folklorist George Lankford has suggested that the group of stories evolved from a single and ancient hunting myth. He believes that the *Djakabish* version is one of the oldest, and probably closest to the original" (Rockwell 2005, 135).

9 For more details, see John Peastitute's *Achan: Naskapi Giant Stories*.

since he sends two lesser-bears as emissaries before confronting Chahkapas himself, as in the first episode of this book.

Still, notwithstanding the scholarship and research that has gone into this question, the contemporary Naskapi and Innu versions of these stories imply that Kachituskw was perceived by the storytellers themselves not as a bear, giant cannibal, or a giant hare, but rather as mammoth-like. During the research for the illustrations commissioned for this volume, we interviewed Naskapi Elders at Kawawachikamach, who confirmed this view. Indeed, the description of the creature by John Peastitute in the storyline itself appears to indicate that Kachituskw was elephant- or mammoth-like. On pages 72/73 we read "Kachituskw lifted him up with its trunk. . ." (*uschûn* 'its nose, snout') and on pages 76/77 Chahkapas tells his sister to make blankets out of the monster's ears.

Regarding our spelling of *Kachituskw*, John Peastitute pronounces this word in the audio recording of the story as *kâ-chî-tûskw*, using three syllables, except for in the song (on pages 70/71), where he sings *Kâ-chî-tu-wâskw*. However, other Naskapi adults pronounce this word *Kâ-chî-tu-wâskw* (with a *w* in the last syllable). The editors decided to use the storyteller's pronunciation, spelling it "Kachituskw" in the English translation and notes, used as a proper name; but writing *Kâchîtuwâskw* in roman transcription and ᑲᒋᑐᐚᔅᒄ in syllabics, reflecting contemporary pronunciation.

Even though similar heroic legends abound in other language groups, the particular rendition of the Chahkapas cycle presented here is distinctly Naskapi and to introduce it properly requires an introduction to the people from whose lips it has been passed from generation to generation for an indeterminate length of time—the Naskapi people themselves. And it is impossible to talk about the Naskapi of today, or those of John Peastitute's time, without saying something of their history.

The Naskapi People

Until the early twentieth century the Naskapi were a loosely affiliated people living in small independent groups, nomadic caribou hunters whose territory spanned the northern portion of the Quebec-Labrador Peninsula. According to Henrikson (2010), the Naskapi probably came together infrequently, perhaps only annually at the peak caribou-hunting season. Until it was closed in 1868, the first principal trading location for the Naskapi was the Petitsikapau post, called Fort Nascopie by the Hudson's Bay Company, situated on the southern extreme of the traditional Naskapi hunting territories. Following the closure of Fort Nascopie, the Naskapi took their business either north to Fort Chimo, or east to the Davis Inlet post, and thus began a process that would eventually lead them to become two separate and sedentary groups. Those who hunted in the northern and northeastern areas of the interior frequented Fort Chimo and Fort McKenzie, and those hunting farther south and east traded at Davis Inlet. Subsequently, each group would adopt distinct Christian traditions, the Eastern Naskapi (Mushuau Innu) becoming Catholics and the Western Naskapi (Naskapi Iyuw) becoming Anglicans.

In 1956, the Fort Chimo (Western) Naskapi journeyed south to the mining town of Schefferville, where educational and medical facilities, as well as employment opportunities in the recently opened iron ore mines, were becoming available (Cooke 2012). A year later they were moved 3 kilometres away from the town to John Lake, where they remained until 1972, along with some Montagnais who had moved to Schefferville from the Sept-Îles area. It was during this period that the Chahkapas cycle along with dozens of other *tipâchimûna* and *atiyûkinch* were performed by John Peastitute and recorded.

In 1969, the Department of Indian and Northern Affairs acquired a 39-acre parcel of land on the north side of Schefferville adjacent to Pearce Lake. By 1972, 106 row-housing units had been built there, forty-three of them for the Naskapi. Most of the Naskapi and Montagnais moved to this site, called the Matimekosh Reserve, but a few families chose to remain at John Lake and are still there to the present time.

In 1978, after several years of negotiations between the Quebec provincial government and Indigenous Peoples of the territory (Inuit, Cree, and Naskapi), the Naskapi signed the Northeastern

Quebec Agreement (Canada 1984), under which they surrendered their claims to land in Quebec in exchange for exclusive rights to *certain* lands and specific social and economic development services to be provided to the Naskapi by the provincial and federal governments.

Of the many things the Northeastern Quebec Agreement provided, one of the most important was in Section 20, which granted the Naskapi the opportunity to move their community to a location and design of their choice. The Naskapi relocated to Kawawachikamach by 1983, about 8 kilometres northeast of the town of Schefferville.

The Naskapi Language

One of the many benefits of self-determination has been the creation of the Naskapi Development Corporation (NDC), which has as one of its stated objectives "to foster, promote, protect, and assist in preserving the Naskapi way of life, values, and traditions" (Quebec 1979). To achieve this aim, the Corporation established their Translation and Linguistics Services Department, which is responsible for carrying out many language development activities for the community, beginning with the Naskapi lexicon and grammar projects. Since 1981, NDC has retained the services of consultant linguists and has trained a team of Naskapi language specialists. To date, a trilingual dictionary (Naskapi-French-English) has been produced (MacKenzie and Jancewicz 1994), and work on elements of a descriptive grammar is underway, along with several other significant language projects.

The Translation and Linguistics Services Department has also undertaken the task of transcribing all the stories recorded with John Peastitute into the Naskapi writing system, with the primary goal of making them available as literature for Naskapi adults and schoolchildren. A secondary goal has been to provide the English literary translations, along with an accessible roman transcription, for people who do not read syllabics. Finally, our analyses of the stories contribute to the growing body of linguistic knowledge about Naskapi that is essential for the grammar and revisions and additions to the dictionary.

In spite of the relatively recent settlement of the Naskapi and Mushuau Innu into different communities, they share family connections that stretch across the Quebec-Labrador Peninsula, and both groups have adopted English as their second language. A unique subset of linguistic features used only by speakers of both language varieties reflects the fact that at one time they constituted a single linguistic group. Among older speakers in particular, there exists a common pool of lexical items, and Eastern and Western Naskapi share a number of phonological and grammatical features (MacKenzie 1980).

But a characteristic difference between Eastern and Western Naskapi worth noting is that Western Naskapi (spoken at Kawawachikamach) is a 'y' dialect while Eastern (Mushuau Innu-aimun) is an 'n' dialect. That is, language varieties that make up the Algonquian language family have been broadly classified by linguists according to the sounds that speakers currently use today for sounds in a reconstructed theoretical "proto" or parent language that these languages are said to have descended from. For example, where a Western Naskapi speaker would say *yutin* (with a 'y') for 'it is windy,' an Innu speaker pronounces this same word *nutin* (with an 'n').

Although in his later years John Peastitute lived in the Western Naskapi community, many features of his speech show that his family affiliations are Eastern, in particular his pronunciation of the Proto-Algonquian *l consonant[10] as 'n' rather than 'y.' A typical example of this can be observed in words like *mi-tâyuwa* 'they are not here' (on pages 60/61). In the recording we hear John pronounce this word *mi-tânuwa*.

In order to make the stories John Peastitute told accessible to readers in Kawawachikamach, in this book the stories have

10 In linguistics, when the form of a certain root or word or phoneme has never been found in a real source, we say it is "unattested." In most proto-languages, <u>all</u> forms are hypothetical; therefore, linguistic convention states that they should be preceded by an asterisk, as with the Proto-Algonquian *l mentioned here.

been written in standard Western Naskapi; that is, those 'n's have been replaced by 'y's, along with some other minor changes to provide transcriptions in standard Kawawachikamach Naskapi. Note, however, that for archival and reference purposes the original recordings which faithfully preserve John Peastitute's exact words and pronunciation are also maintained by the Translation and Linguistics Services Department.

Recording the Stories

In 1967 and 1968, Serge Melançon visited the John Lake community near Schefferville to record stories on tape. He was working with the Laboratoire d'anthropologie amérindienne under the supervision of Rémi Savard, on a project to collect oral traditions of several Quebec groups and to compare the content and style of the similar stories across linguistic and cultural boundaries. Savard's book *Carcajou et le sens du monde: récits Montagnais-Naskapi* (Savard 1971) is one of the results of that project and is a worthwhile reference companion to this volume. Interested readers would do well to consult it for a thorough analysis of some of the other stories told by several First Nations in Quebec.

From Tape to Book

The collection of Innu and Naskapi tapes that were originally collected by Savard's project remained the property of the Laboratoire, but copies on cassette tape were later released to linguists for eventual transcription. Many of the Sheshatshiu Innu stories from this project are available online at innu-aimun.ca and as printed books (Lefebvre, Lanari, and Mailhot 1999).

Following the completion of Savard's project, copies of the Naskapi tapes, along with photocopies of some of the transcriptions, were placed at the NDC office located in Schefferville at the time.

In the course of the compilation of the Naskapi Lexicon, the NDC board decided to also take on the task of transcribing and translating the stories as a cultural development project.

Since the quality of the copies at the NDC office was poor, in the early 1990s Marguerite MacKenzie began to track down the original tapes to obtain access to better-quality recordings. She worked with Bill Jancewicz, a linguist affiliated with SIL International, who had moved to Kawawachikamach with his family and had just been invited to serve as NDC's linguistics resource person. With Bill's help, NDC translators Philip "B" Einish and Thomas Sandy skimmed and annotated the photocopied material. Some of this material had been typed, some handwritten. Some were photocopies of Melançon's or others' field notes, and some were preliminary transcriptions of the tapes made by Elijah Einish in the early 1980s. Some of the photocopied pages had been keyboarded by Marguerite or one of her students at Memorial University in the late 1980s. All of this material, amounting to several hundred pages, was examined by Bill, Phil, and Thomas in an attempt to match existing Naskapi transcriptions with their respective translations. Still, there remained a good deal of uncertainty about many of these pages even after this task was completed.

In April of 1994, Bill visited José Mailhot, one of the curators of the collection, in Montreal. She and co-curator Sylvie Vincent agreed to produce new copies of the original audio recordings for the project, with the following conditions:

- They agreed to release the 1967 material only, comprising eight tapes, as the quality of those tapes was much better than the 1968 tapes.

- Copies were to be produced by professionals in Montreal so that the originals would not be circulated. They also provided a listing of the tape contents.

- The tapes could be used provided that mention be made (in any publication) that the source audio material is owned by the Laboratoire d'anthropologie amérindienne, and that the copies of the tapes eventually be donated to "the Naskapi Band of

> Schefferville through their school or their cultural centre if they [had] one."

We have interpreted this final condition with the understanding that the Naskapi Development Corporation fills the role of "cultural centre" and handles language material archiving and distribution on behalf of the rest of the community. Eight compact cassettes (copies of the originals) were thus received by the Corporation from the Laboratoire in 1994.

During August and September of 1994, Bill listened to all the tapes and compared the content with the pages and pages of documentation, then produced an inventory of all the stories, their (presumed) titles, position in the audio collection, and all associated documentation.

Both the list that was provided with the tapes and many of the handwritten notes had been marked with a code number that was implemented in the original Laboratoire project. These codes are still used as the principal means of identifying the various stories. The story inventory is keyed to the original tape cassette (side A or side B) and counter number (specific to the tape-recording machine used to originally tabulate the volumes). The tape volume number corresponds to *one side* of the tape in question. Some tapes were not recorded on both sides. Consequently, the eight cassettes in the possession of NDC comprise the fourteen volumes ("sides") listed in the inventory. This part of the collection includes stories referenced 1 through 36, recorded in 1967. Stories 37 through 59 were recorded in 1968, and the audio quality of these recordings is less than optimal. The titles given were derived from the one provided on the original tape inventory and/or the title listed on one or more of the transcriptions. The genre classification provided in the inventory indicates whether the story is considered a "legend" or myth (*âtiyûhkin*) or a "true account" (*tipâchimûn*). Sometimes this is clear from the content: for example, stories about animals that talk are generally accepted to be *âtiyûhkinch,* but occasionally a story that might be identified as a myth by some (because it may have supernatural events, for example) is classified as a *tipâchimûn* by John Peastitute himself. We have retained the storyteller's classification of all the stories in the collection.

Shortly after receiving the new copies of the tapes from the curators of the collection in October 1994, Phil, Thomas, and Bill listened together to one story (number 24, "The Dancing Ants"), and the text was carefully transcribed from the audio into syllabics by Thomas and then into roman by Bill. Next, Bill keyboarded the text into the computer and Thomas proofread this transcription. Later, Phil provided a rough English translation of the story. This was the first story translation completed by the department.

In the spring of 1995, after listening to and transcribing about a dozen of the stories by hand in syllabics, Thomas Sandy left his position at NDC for personal reasons. That summer, the NDC head office relocated to Kawawachikamach. Early in 1996, Alma Chemaganish was hired to replace Thomas, and she began listening to the tapes and transcribing the stories into syllabics. This time, however, the transcription was done directly to computer.

Later, Alma would read the story off the computer screen to Phil, who translated what he heard and then keyboarded the English version into another computer.

Current Project Status

Since that time, under the supervision of the linguistic consultants (Dr. Marguerite MacKenzie and Dr. Julie Brittain) and assisted by NDC's linguistics resource person (Bill Jancewicz), the analytical procedures evolved to include adding paragraph breaks, punctuation, line numbering, combining the Naskapi transcription with the English translation, back-translation, linguistic analysis charting, and interlinear morpheme analysis. After this analysis, a thorough revision of the story text and English translation is done.

Some of the stories in the collection have also been selected for discourse analysis. These procedures help the linguists to understand the structures of Naskapi storytelling style for each story genre, as well as insight into the character, motivation, and personality of the Naskapi storyteller.

An important step was taken late in 1999 with regard to preservation of these oral histories. It has been demonstrated in recent years that magnetic audio tapes inevitably degrade and lose their sound quality over the years, rendering them difficult to hear or even completely useless. The NDC language department therefore contracted an audio specialist to transfer the tapes to digital media and to enhance the sound quality of all the stories in their collection. This has preserved the precious Naskapi legacy of these oral histories that date back to the 1960s. Since that time, additional steps have been incorporated in the handling of these audio files, including digitally editing these stories to remove distracting noises and errors, dividing the various stories into separate audio files, annotating the audio files to match the numbering of the text files, and producing digital copies, audio CDs, and MP3 files for analysis, broadcasting, and general use.

Literary Translation Process

While our primary goal has always been to render the stories in the Naskapi writing system so that they would be accessible to current Naskapi readers in Kawawachikamach, a secondary goal has been to reproduce in English the elegance and stylistic skill employed by the storyteller while remaining as faithful as possible to the original text.

Wherever possible, we have tried to mirror the techniques used in the original Naskapi. For example, we have replicated in English the use of the Naskapi diminutive forms when they are used to refer to Chahkapas as a small person. This occurs on pages 68/69 when Chahkapas lies down to wait for Kachituskw. The Naskapi reads: *Âku nâtâ tâhkûch nâtâ âkutâ pâmisîhk. Pâmisinist.* The final words in that line are from the verb *pimisin* 'lie down'; the last word has the diminutive ending *-ist.* We have translated this with the words 'The little guy lay down.'

The translation process we adopted involved several stages. Besides the procedures described in the section From Tape to

Book above, these additional steps were followed: In group sessions the digital audio file of each story was listened to line by line, while the Naskapi team followed along, reading a transcribed version in syllabics which was projected on a screen for the group to see. Each word of the transcription was verified for accuracy and faithfulness to the performance, and translated into a fairly literal rendering. Each verb was also parsed for its inflectional morphology, and the Naskapi team was asked about accurate translation, natural expression, and cultural matters.

As each story was thus meticulously annotated, reviewed, and corrected, careful notes were kept with the transcription and translation. These notes were then turned over to Dr. Julie Brittain, a specialist in Algonquian syntax as well as a gifted translator of Naskapi, with the ability not only to capture the meaning of the original story but also to communicate something of the style of the story based on her study of Naskapi language structures. If any questions arose during this stage, these were once again reviewed by the Naskapi team at Kawawachikamach before the text was passed on for formatting, typesetting, and design. Illustrations were also commissioned at this stage. After this work was completed, a proof copy was provided to the editors and the translation team. The annotated Naskapi transcription and the literary English translation were then reviewed a final time along with the accompanying illustrations.

The final publication is professionally designed so that readers from the various target audiences can once again appreciate the storyteller's craft, whether they are accomplished readers of Naskapi, young Naskapi students, casual readers, or students of Algonquian literature.

References and Recommended Further Reading

Bird, Louis. 2007. *Spirit Lives in the Mind: Omushkego Stories, Lives, and Dreams*. Montreal: McGill-Queen's University Press.

Brittain, Julie, and Marguerite MacKenzie. 2004. "Umâyichîs." Pp. 572–90 in *Voices from Four Directions: Contemporary Translations of the Native Literatures of North America*. Lincoln, NE: University of Nebraska Press.

———. 2005. "Two Wolverine Stories." Pp. 121–58 in *Algonquian Spirit: Contemporary Translations of the Native Literatures of North America*. Lincoln, NE: University of Nebraska Press.

———. 2011. "Translating Algonquian Oral Texts." Pp. 242–74 in *Born in the Blood: On Native American Translation*. Lincoln, NE: University of Nebraska Press.

Canada, Government of. 1975. "James Bay and Northern Quebec Agreement (JBNQA)." Ottawa, ON: Department of Indian Affairs and Northern Development. http://extwprlegs1.fao.org/docs/pdf/que136636.pdf.

———. 1984. "Northeastern Quebec Agreement (NEQA)." Ottawa, ON: Department of Indian Affairs and Northern Development. http://extwprlegs1.fao.org/docs/pdf/que136635.pdf.

Desbarats, Peter. 1969. *What They Used to Tell about: Indian Legends from Labrador*. Toronto, ON: McClelland & Stewart.

Ellis, C. Douglas. 1989. *"Now Then, Still Another Story": Literature of the Western James Bay Cree: Content and Structure*. Winnipeg, MB: Voices of Rupert's Land.

Henriksen, Georg. 2010. *Hunters in the Barrens: The Naskapi on the Edge of the White Man's World*. New York: Berghahn Books.

Lankford, George E. 1980. "Pleistocene Animals in Folk Memory." *The Journal of American Folklore* 93(369) (July 1): 293–304. doi:10.2307/540573. http://www.jstor.org/stable/540573.

Lefebvre, Madeleine. 1974. *Tshakapesh, récits montagnais-naskapis*. 2nd ed. Cultures Amérindiennes 4. Québec, QC: Ministère des Affaires culturelles / Éditeur officiel du Québec.

Lefebvre, Madeleine, Robert Lanari, José Mailhot, and Labrador Innu Text Project. *Sheshatshiu-Atanukana Mak Tipatshimuna*. Labrador Innu Text Project, 1999. https://collections.mun.ca/digital/collection/innu.

MacKenzie, Marguerite. 1980. "Towards a Dialectology of Cree-Montagnais-Naskapi." PhD thesis (dissertation), Department of Linguistics, University of Toronto. http://resources.atlas-ling.ca/wp-content/uploads/2015/02/MMacKenzie-Towards-a-Dialectology-of-Cree-Montagnais-Naskapi.pdf.

MacKenzie, Marguerite, and Bill Jancewicz. 1994. *Naskapi Lexicon / Lexique Naskapi*. First Edition. 3 vols. Kawawachikamach, QC: Naskapi Development Corporation.

Michelson, Truman. 1936. "Mammoth or 'Stiff-Legged Bear'." *American Anthropologist* 38(1) (January 1): 141–143. doi:10.2307/662559. http://www.jstor.org/stable/662559.

Morris, Jemima. 1989. "Chaka-Pesh and the Moon Legend." *Canadian Woman Studies* 10(2) (September 1). https://cws.journals.yorku.ca/index.php/cws/article/view/11174/10263.

Parkman, Francis. 1871. *The Conspiracy of Pontiac and the Indian War after the Conquest of Canada*. Boston, MA: Harvard University Press.

Peastitute, John. 2013. *Kuihkwahchaw: Naskapi Wolverine Legends*. Edited by Marguerite MacKenzie. Translated by Julie Brittain. Kawawachikamach, QC: Naskapi Development Corporation.

———. 2015. *Achan: Naskapi Giant Stories*. Edited by Marguerite MacKenzie. Translated by Julie Brittain. Kawawachikamach, QC: Naskapi Development Corporation.

Quebec, National Assembly of. 1979. "An Act Respecting the Naskapi Development Corporation." Québec, QC: Publications du Québec. http://www2.publicationsduquebec.gouv.qc.ca/dynamicSearch/telecharge.php?type=2&file=//S_10_1/S10_1_A.htm.

Randall, Catharine. 2011. *Black Robes and Buckskin: A Selection from the Jesuit "Relations."* New York: Fordham University Press.

Rockwell, David B. 2003. *Giving Voice to Bear: North American Indian Myths, Rituals, and Images of the Bear*. Lanham, MD: Roberts Rinehart: Distributed by National Book Network.

Savard, Rémi. 1971. *Carcajou et le sens du monde: récits Montagnais-Naskapi*. Troisième édition revue et corrigée edition. Civilisation du Québec 3. Éditeur Officiel du Québec, Québec. http://classiques.uqac.ca/contemporains/savard_remi/carcajou/carcajou.html.

———. 1985. *La Voix des Autres*. Positions anthropologiques. Montréal: L'Hexagone. http://classiques.uqac.ca/contemporains/savard_remi/voix_des_autres/voix_des_autres.html.

Schoolcraft, Henry Rowe. 1839. *Algic Researches: Indian Tales and Legends*. Vol. I & II. 2 vols. New York: Harper & Brothers.

Scott, Simeon. 1995. *Cree Legends and Narratives from the West Coast of James Bay: Âtalôhkâna Nêsta Tipâcimôwina*. Translated by C. Douglas Ellis. Publications of the Algonquian

Text Society. Winnipeg, MB: University of Manitoba Press. http://uofmpress.ca/books/detail/cree-legends-and-narratives-from-the-west-coast-of-james-bay.

Siebert, F.T., Jr. 1937. "Mammoth or 'Stiff-Legged Bear'." *American Anthropologist* 39(4) (October 1): 721–725. doi:10.2307/662451. http://www.jstor.org/stable/662451.

Speck, Frank G. 1935. "Mammoth or 'Stiff-Legged Bear'." *American Anthropologist* 37(1) (January 1): 159–163. doi:10.2307/662250. http://www.jstor.org/stable/662250.

Strong, W.D. 1934. "North American Indian Traditions Suggesting a Knowledge of the Mammoth." *American Anthropologist* 36(1) (January 1): 81–88. doi:10.2307/661759. http://www.jstor.org/stable/661759.

Thwaites, Reuben Gold. 1896. *The Jesuit Relations and Allied Documents: Travels and Explorations of the Jesuit Missionaries in New France, 1610–1791.* Vol. 11. 71 vols. Cleveland, OH: Burrows Bros. http://moses.creighton.edu/kripke/jesuitrelations/relations_01.html.

Contributors and Collaborators

On behalf of the Naskapi people, the Naskapi Development Corporation would like to thank those who contributed to making this volume possible.

Dr. Julie Brittain is an associate professor in the Department of Linguistics at Memorial University, Newfoundland. She began research on the dialect of Naskapi spoken at Kawawachikamach in 1996 and continues to work on this and related dialects. She is the author of *The Morphosyntax of the Algonquian Conjunct Verb: A Minimalist Approach* (2001) and has written numerous articles on the structure of Cree, Innu-aimun, and Naskapi.

Alma Chemaganish is a member of the Naskapi Nation of Kawawachikamach. She worked for the Naskapi Development Corporation as a Naskapi translator and proofreader. She has contributed to the translation and editing of the collection of Naskapi stories and legends that the selections in this volume are a part of, and served as the main copyeditor for corporation documents in Naskapi.

Philip "B" Einish was Chief of the Naskapi Nation of Kawawachikamach for three terms since 1997. He served as the coordinator of the Naskapi Development Corporation Translation and Linguistics Services Department, a position he has held for more than two decades. He has been a visionary and catalyst for preserving the Naskapi language and culture in his community.

Bill Jancewicz is a member of SIL International and Wycliffe Bible Translators, and has served the Naskapi community in language development with his wife, Norma Jean, since 1988. He has worked with the Naskapi Development Corporation as a linguistics resource person since 1992, providing technical support for Naskapi language development, training, and facilitation in translation and literature production. He is coeditor of the *Naskapi Lexicon* (1994) and the *East Cree Lexicon: Eastern James Bay Dialects* (2004), and project coordinator for the NDC's series of John Peastitute stories.

Elizabeth Jancewicz grew up in Schefferville and Kawawachikamach, arriving with her family there when she was just one year old. After attending the Naskapi school, she studied art at Norwich Free Academy in Connecticut and Houghton College in New York. She returned to the Naskapi community in 2010 to teach art at the Naskapi school. As part of the touring band *Pocket Vinyl*, she serves as the visual arts component of the creative team. She continues to illustrate a growing collection of children's books and graphic novels. www.pocketvinyl.com.

Dr. Marguerite MacKenzie has served as professor and head of the Department of Linguistics at Memorial University, Newfoundland, and has spent her career working with speakers of Cree, Innu (Montagnais), and Naskapi on dictionaries, grammars, and language training materials. She is coeditor of the *East Cree Lexicon: Eastern James Bay Dialects* (2004, 2012), the *Naskapi Lexicon* (1994) and the English and French versions of the *Innu Lexicon* (2013). She is presently involved in a collaborative research project to investigate language assessment tools for Innu students.

Silas Nabinicaboo is a member of the Naskapi Nation of Kawawachikamach. He is trained as a Naskapi translator and interpreter and worked for the Naskapi Development Corporation as a Naskapi language editor and technician. He is the editor of the *Naskapi Hymn Book* (1999) and the lead translator for the *Naskapi New Testament* (2007). He has served for many years as lay reader for Naskapi scriptures at St. John's Church, Kawawachikamach, and has recently been ordained deacon by Bishop Dennis Drainville, Diocese of Quebec.

John Peastitute (1896–1981) was a Naskapi Elder who was well respected not only as a story-keeper, but also as a storyteller. His repertoire of both *tipâchimûna* and *âtiyûhkinch* was extensive, and his performances engaging. He had an extensive knowledge of the traditional Naskapi life. His children, grandchildren and great-grandchildren still live in Kawawachikamach. His stories, many of which are aired on the Naskapi radio program *Voices of our Grandfathers*, are much loved and treasured by all generations.

ᓇᔅᑲᐱ ᐃᔪᐤ ᐃᔨᒧᐅᓐ ᐊᐃᓯ ᒥᓯᓇᐃᒐᓄᐅᒡ

Naskapi Syllabic Chart

i / *ii*	ᐃ	*u* / *uu*	ᐅ	*a* / *aa*	ᐊ						
wi / *wii*	ᐏ			*wa* / *waa*	ᐙ	*w*	ᐤ				
pi / *pii*	ᐱ	*pu* / *puu*	ᐳ	*pa* / *paa*	ᐸ	*p*	ᑉ	*pwaa*	ᐹ		
ti / *tii*	ᑎ	*tu* / *tuu*	ᑐ	*ta* / *taa*	ᑕ	*t*	ᑦ	*twaa*	ᑘ		
ki / *kii*	ᑭ	*ku* / *kuu*	ᑯ	*ka* / *kaa*	ᑲ	*k*	ᒃ	*kwaa*	ᑻ	*kw*	ᑿ
chi / *chii*	ᒋ	*chu* / *chuu*	ᒍ	*cha* / *chaa*	ᒐ	*ch*	ᒡ	*chwaa*	ᒞ		
mi / *mii*	ᒥ	*mu* / *muu*	ᒧ	*ma* / *maa*	ᒪ	*m*	ᒻ	*mwaa*	ᒷ		
ni / *nii*	ᓂ	*nu* / *nuu*	ᓄ	*na* / *naa*	ᓇ	*n*	ᓐ	*nwaa*	ᓏ		
si / *sii*	ᓯ	*su* / *suu*	ᓱ	*sa* / *saa*	ᓴ	*s*	ᔅ	*swaa*	ᓵ		
yi / *yii*	ᔨ	*yu* / *yuu*	ᔪ	*ya* / *yaa*	ᔭ	*y*	ᔾ	*ywaa*	ᔮ		

Other Symbols:

Long and short vowels are not distinguished in written Naskapi. In this book, long vowels are written in the roman text with a circumflex accent (hat), thus: *kaa* = *kâ* (long), *ka* (short); either one written simply ᑲ in syllabics.

The symbol ᔅ followed by ᐹ ᑘ ᑻ or ᒞ can be written as a contraction, thus: *spwaa* ᐹ *stwaa* ᑘ *skwaa* ᑻ and *schwaa* ᒞ.

Pre-aspirated "soft" *hk* (often pronounced as a "hard" *h*) may be written with a single dot, as in: *hki* ᑮ *hku* ᑰ *hkaa* ᑳ.

English-style punctuation is used throughout, except for the full stop or period, which is ᙮ in Naskapi.

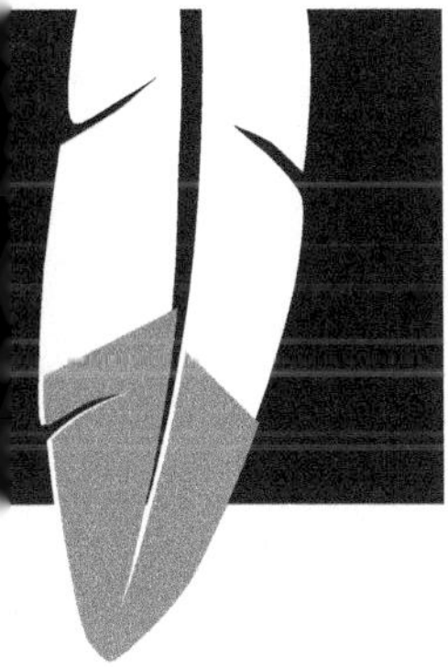

ᒐᐧᑲᐸᐣ

1. ᒐᐧᑲᐸᐢ ᑭᔭ ᑲᒋᑐᐋᐢᒄ

ᐊᑯ ᐊᐣ ᐃᔨᐤ ᐊᑕᑦ ᐊᐣᑕ, ᒥᒄ ᐅᑕᓂᐢ ᐏᒋᒪᐤ, ᑭᔭ ᐏᐋ, ᑭᔭ ᐏᐩ, ᓂᐢᑐᐅᐠ᙮

ᐊᑯ ᐃᑕᐤ, ᓂᔭᔨᐋ ᐅᑕᓂᐢ, "ᓂᑭ ᐃᔭᐣ ᒪ ᐊᑯ ᓂᑭ ᐏ ᐅᓯᑕᐣ ᐊᐣ ᒋᑦ ᐅᐤᑎᓄᐤ," ᐃᑕᐤ᙮

"ᐅᐢᑯᔭ ᐊᐣᑕ ᑕᔨᐋ ᐊᐣᑕ ᐱᐢᑯᑎᓇᐠ ᐊᐣᑕ; ᐊᐅᑯᐤ ᐊᐣᐠ ᒐ ᓇᑎᒋᐠ," ᐃᑕᐤ᙮

"ᓂᑭ ᒥᓂᐧᑯᒧᐣ," ᐃᑕᐤ᙮ "ᓂᑭ ᐅᓯᑕᐣ ᐅᐢᑯᐅᐤᑦ," ᐃᑕᐤ, "ᒐ ᐅᑦ ᐅᐤᑎᔭᐧᒄ," ᐃᑕᐤ᙮

"ᓂᐦᐃ," ᐃᑎᑯᐤ᙮

ᐊᑯ ᓂᔭᔨᐋ ᐏᐋ, "ᐏᒐᐏ," ᐃᑕᐤ᙮

ᒐᑐᑕᐠ, ᐋᒐᐋᑦ᙮

ᐊᑯ ᐊᓐ ᐃᔅ:ᑲᔅ ᐧᐃᒋᐋᐤ ᐊᓂᔭ ᑲᓄᐋᔨᑕᐧᒃ᙮

ᐊᑯ ᒥ ᑕᔪᐋ ᐊᑎ ᐅᑕᑯᓯᔨᒡ ᐅᑕᐧᐃᔭ᙮ ᐊᑎ ᓂᑐᐋᐱᒪᑦ, ᒪᐋᒡ᙮ ᐊᑯ ᐊᓐ ᐃᔅ:ᑲᐤ ᒋ ᑕᔪᐋ ᐅᑦ ᐊᐋᓯᒪ᙮ ᐊᔅᒄ ᒥ ᐅᒋ ᐃᔪᐤ, ᐃᔪᐤ, ᒥ ᐅᒋ ᐃᔪᐤ, ᐊᐅᑯᓐ ᐊᓐ ᒐᐧᑲᐸᔅ ᒐ ᐃᓯᓂᐧᑲᑕᑭᓄᐅᑦ, ᐊᓐ ᐊᐋᔅ ᐊᓐ ᒐ ᐃᔪᑦ᙮

ᐊᑯ ᓂᔭᔪᐋ ᑲᒋᑐᐋᔅᒄ ᐃᓯᓂᐧᑲᑕᑭᓂᔪᐋ᙮ ᐊᐅᑯᓂ ᐋᑎᑎᑯᒡ, ᓇᐸᐃᑯᒡ᙮

ᐊᑯ ᒧᑯᒡ ᑭᔫ ᓇᐸᐃᑯᒡ᙮ ᐊᑯ ᐊᓐ ᒐᐧᑲᐸᔅ ᐊᑕᑭᓄᐅᑦ, ᓇᑕᐅᒋᑦ ᐊᓐ ᐊᐋᔅ᙮

ᒥ ᒧᑯᐤ᙮ ᒥᒄ ᓂᔭᔪᐤ ᒥᓂᐱᑎᑯᐤ ᓂᔭᔪᐤ, ᓂᔭᔪᐤ ᐊᓐᑕ ᐊᑕᑦ ᐊ ᓂᑕᐅᒋᑦ, ᒪᓇᑕ ᐧᐃᔭᐱᓂᑯᑦ᙮ ᐊᑯ ᓂᔭᔪᐋ ᐅᑲᐧᐃᔭ ᒥᒄ ᒧᐋᔨᒋ ᑭᔭ ᓂᔭᔪᐋ ᐅᑕᐧᐃᔭ; ᒥ ᑕᔪᐋ᙮

ᐊᑯ ᒐᒃ ᓇᔅᒡ ᐊᑎ ᐅᑕᑯᓯᔨᒡ ᓇᔅᒡ᙮ “ᓂᑭ ᓂᑐᐋᐱᒪᐅᒡ ᒪ ᐊᑯ ᓄᑕᐧᐃᔾ,” ᐃᑕᔨᑎᒻ ᐊᓐ ᐃᔅ:ᑲᔅ᙮ ᒐᑐᑕᑦ ᓇᑐᐋᐱᒪᑦ᙮

ᐊᐅᑯᓂ ᐅᔭᔪᐋ ᐊᓐᑕ ᐋᑎᑎ:ᒪᑦ ᓇᐸᐃᑯᔨ:ᑲᓂ ᐅᑕ ᐊᐋᔪᐋ᙮ ᐅᑲᐧᐃᔭ ᓇᔅᑎᔅ ᐊᓐᑕ ᒥ ᐃᔅᑯᐳᑯᔪᐋ ᒐ:ᑲᓐ᙮ “ᓴᔅ ᓂᔭᐧᑲ ᓂᐸᐃᑯᓯᐱᓂᒡ ᐊᐋᔪᐋ,” ᐃᑕᔨᒪᐤ᙮

ᐊᑯ ᓂᔭᔪᐤ ᑭ ᓇᓂᑐᐋᐳᐋ :ᑲ ᐃᑎᑦ ᐊᓐ ᐃᔅ:ᑲᔅ ᓇᑕ ᐊ ᓯᓯᐧᐃ:ᑲᑯᓂᑲᔨᒡ ᓂᔭᔪᐋ ᑭᔫ ᒐ:ᑲᓂᔪᐤ ᓂᔭᔪᐤ᙮ ᐧᐃᔭᐸᑕᐧᒃ ᓇᑕ ᐋᔅᒐᒋᑯᓇᔨᒡ ᒐ:ᑲᓂᔪᐤ᙮ ᓂᔭᑕᐧᒃ, ᐋᑎᓇᐧᒃ᙮ ᐊᐅᑯᓂ, ᓇᔅᑐᓄᐋᑦ ᐊᐋᓴ ᐊᓐᑕ ᐊᑕᔨᒋ᙮ ᐋᑎᓇᑦ, ᐱᔭᐧᑲᐱᑎ:ᒪᑦ ᓂᔭᔪᐋ ᐊᑕᔨᒋ᙮

ᐊᐅᑯᐤ ᐊᐋᓯᔅ ᐊᓐᑕ ᐊᑕᓯᑦ᙮ ᒥ ᐱᑯᐱᑎᑯᐤ ᑕᓐᑕ᙮
“ᐧᐋᔅ ᐊᐅᑯᐤ ᓂᓯᒼ ᑲ ᑕᑦ,” ᐃᑕᔨᒪᐤ ᐊᓐ ᐃᔅ:ᑲᔅ᙮

ᐊᑯ, “ᑕᓐᑕ ᓂᐸ ᒋ ᐅᒋ ᐃᔨᐱᒐᓐ?”

ᐊᑯ ᐊᓐ ᐊᐋᓯᔅ ᐋᑎᓇᑦ ᐊᓂᔦᐋ ᐅᓯᒪ, ᐊᑯ ᐊᓐᑕ ᐊᑎ ᐃᔭᓯᑦ ᐊᓐᑕ ᒐ:ᑲᓂᔦᐤ, ᒋ ᑕᐧᑯᓂᒼ ᒐ:ᑲᓂᔦᐤ᙮ ᐊᔅᒋᐧᑯᓯᔦᐤ ᐊᑯᑕ ᑲ ᑕᐧᑯᓇᐧᒃ, ᐊᐅᑯᔦᐤ ᓂᔭᔦᐤ ᐸᑕᐋᑦ ᓂᔭᔦᐋ ᐊᐋᓯᓴ᙮ ᐊᑯ ᑲ ᐱᑕᐋᑦ ᐊᑯᐧ ᔭᔭᒋᓯᔨᒋ ᓂᔭᔦᐋ ᐊᐋᓴ᙮ ᒐᐱᒋᐋᐋᓯᑦ ᓂᔭᔦᐤ ᒋᐱᒋᐋᐃᑭᓂᔦᐤ᙮

ᐊᑯ ᒐᐋᑕᐊᑦ᙮

ᐊᑯ ᓇᑕ ᑲ ᑎᑯᓯᑕᐊᑦ ᐊᑯ ᒋᒋᐋ ᒐ:ᓴᔭᒋᔨᒋ, ᔭᔭᒋᓯᔨᒋ᙮

ᐊᑯ ᑲᓄᐋᔨᒪᑦ ᐅᓯᒪ᙮

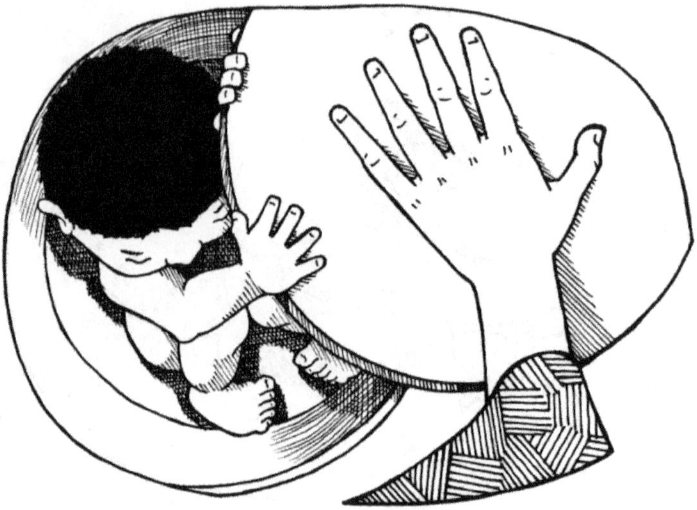

“ᑕᓐᑕ ᓂᐸᒋ ᐅᒋ ᐃᔨᐱᒐᓐ?” ᐃᑕᔨᑎᒼ᙮

ᐊᑯ ᓂᔭᔪᐤ ᒐᐠ ᓂᔭᔪᐤ ᐅᑦ ᐊᐢᒋᐧᑯ ᓂᔭᔪᐤ, ᐊᑯᑕ ᐊᓐᑕ ᐊᑎ ᐃᔭᓯᑦ, ᐊᓐᑕ ᐅᑦ ᐊᐢᒋᐧᑯᒡ᙮ ᐱᔭᓂᒍᐚᐢᑭᒥᔨᒋ ᓂᔭᔪᐤ ᐅᑦ ᐊᐢᒋᐧᑯ; ᒪᓯᑎᔨᒋ, ᒪᓯᑎᓯᔨᒋ ᒐᐠ᙮ ᐚᐚᒡ, ᐚᐚᒡ ᒋᒋᐚ ᒐᐠ ᒋᔨᐱᒍᐤ ᐊᓐ ᐊᐚᐢ᙮

ᐊᑯ ᐊᑎ ᒥᓯᑎᓯᑦ, ᐊᑎ ᓂᑕᐚᔨᒋ᙮ ᒼᒼᒼ᙮

• • •

“ᓂᒥᓴ,” ᐃᑕᐤ᙮ ᓴᐢ ᑭᐹ :ᑲ ᒋᐢᒐᔨᒪᑦ᙮

“ᓇᓯ,” ᑭᐹ ᐃᑕᒐ ᒧᓯᓇᐤ᙮

“ᓂᒥᓴ,” ᐃᑕᐤ, “ᑕᓐᑕ ᒪ ᐚᒋ ᓂᑕᐅᒋᔭᐧᑯ ᐊᑲ ᒍᑕᐧᐃᓇᓄᐚ ᑭᔭ ᐊᑲ ᒋᑲᐧᐃᓇᓄᐚ?” ᐃᑕᐤ᙮

“ᐊᐅᑯᐤ ᓇᓯ, ᐚᐢ ᓂᔭᐧᑲ ᐊᓐᒡ ᒍᑕᐧᐃᓄᐤ ᑭᔭ

ᑭᑲᐑᓄᐤ, ᑭ ᓂᐸᐃᑯᒡ ᐊᐚᔪᐚ,” ᐃᑕᐤ᙮ “ᐊᑯ ᑕᒥᒡ ᐊᓐᑕ ᐢᑭ ᐃᑕᓐ ᑭᑲᐑᓄᐤ ᐅᔭᒡ,” ᐃᑕᐤ᙮ “ᐊᑯ ᐊᐢᐠ ᒥ ᑭ ᐅᑭ ᐃᔪᓐ, ᐊᑯ ᓇᐸᐃᑯᒡ ᐊᐚᔪᐚ᙮ ᐊᑯ ᒥ ᑭ ᐱᒪᒋᒥᑯᓯᐱᓐ ᓂᔭᔪᐚ ᑲ ᓂᐸᐃᑯᒡ, ᑭ ᐚᐱᓂᑯᓯᐱᓐ ᐊᓐᑕ᙮

ᓇᑐᐚᐱᒥᑕᓐ, ᒪᐢᑲᑕᓐ,” ᐃᑕᐤ, “ᐊᑯ ᒐᐚᑕᐃᑕᓐ,” ᐃᑕᐤ᙮ ᐚᑎᒧᐚᐟ ᐊᓂᔭ ᐊ ᑐᑐᐚᐟ ᐅᓯᒪ᙮

“ᓂᐦᐃ,” ᐃᑎᑯᐤ᙮

ᐸᑐᐢ ᒐᐢᒐᒋᑕᐧᐠ ᐊᓐ ᐊᐚᐢ᙮ ᒼᒼᒼ᙮

•••

“ᓂᒥᓴ, ᓂᑫ ᒥᑎᓴᓂᑿᓱᓐ ᒪ,” ᐃᑕᐤ᙮

ᒼᒼᒼ᙮ ᒐ ᐃᑎ:ᑲ ᑕᐸ ᑭ ᑫᐢᑐᑎᑯᐤ ᐅᒥᓴ᙮ ᒪᑎᓴᓂᑿᓱᐟ᙮ ᒼᒼᒼ᙮ ᐸᒐᐟ᙮

ᑕᔦ̇, ᐸᐸᑕᑯᓱᒡ ᐊᓐᑕ ᐅᒥᑎᓴᓂᒡ; ᐊᓐᑕ ᒪᒍᒋᐧᑭᓱᒡ᙮ ᐊᑯ ᒐᒃ, “ᐊᐦᐊᑲ, ᓂᒥᓴ, ᐱᑯᓇ, ᐱᑯᓇ!”

ᐸᑯᐱᑎᒥᔪᒋ ᐅᔭᔦᐋ ᐅᒥᓴ ᐅᒥᑎᓴᓐ᙮ ᒋ ᐊᑯᓇᐊᒻ :ᑲ ᑐᑕᑭᓄᐅᒡ ᒥᑎᓴᓐ ᐊᓯᓂᐧᑲᑕᒡ᙮

ᐊᐅᑯᐤ ᐊᐱᐨ, ᓴᐢ ᒥᓯᑐᐤ᙮ ᒥ ᐃᓯᓇᑯᓱᐤ ᓂᔭᔦᐤ ᑲ ᐃᓯᓇᑯᐢᐨ ᑲ ᐃᐢᐱᑎᐢᐨ᙮ ᓇᐊᒻ ᐃᔦᐋ ᐊᐢᐱᑎᔪᒋ ᓴᐢ :ᑲ ᐃᐢᐱᑎᐨ ᐊ ᐃᓯᓇᑯᐅᐨ᙮

ᒥ ᑭᐢᑐᑎᑯᐤ ᐃᔭᐱᒡ ᐅᒥᓴ; ᑕᓐ ᒋᐸ ᐃᑎᑯᐤ?

ᐊᑯ ᒐᒃ, ᐋᔦᐧᐃᐨ ᒋᔭᒋᓴᐸᔭᔪᒡ᙮ ᒻᒻᒻ᙮

“ᓂᒥᓴ,” ᐃᑕᐤ, “ᓂᑭ ᐃᔭᓐ ᒪ,” ᐃᑕᐤ᙮ “ᓂᑭ ᒥᓂᑲᐋᐅᒡ ᒪ ᓂᑭᐢᑯᒡ ᑭᔭ ᓂᑦ ᐊᒐᐱᔾ,” ᐃᑕᐤ᙮

ᒥᒄ ᐊᐱᓯᓱᐤ, ᒥ ᓇᐢᒡ ᐃᐢᐱᑐᐤ ᐃᔦᐋ ᐊᐢᐱᑎᔪᒋ᙮ ᒥᒄ ᓱᒐᔪᑕᑯᓱᐤ, ᒥᒄ ᑭᒐᒋᑐᐤ ᒋᒋᐋ᙮

“ᓂᐦᐃ,” ᐃᑎᑯᐤ᙮

ᐊᑯ ᒐᑐᑕᐨ᙮

ᐊᑯ ᓂᔭᔦᐋ ᐋᒋᓇᑭᓇᑎ:ᑲ ᐊ ᒥ:ᔭᐢᑯᓯᔪᒋ ᒥᒄ ᐱᐱᒋᑲᐋᐤ, ᒻᒻᒻ, ᑭᔦ̇ ᒐᓇ̈ᐢ:ᑲᐊᐨ᙮

ᐊᑯ ᓂᔭᔦᐋ, ᓂᔭᔦᐋ ᒥᐢᑎ:ᑲ ᓄᑎᒪᐢᑯᓯᔪᒋ ᐃᔭᑎ:ᑲ᙮ ᐊᐅᑯᓂ ᐊ̈ ᐅᑭᐢᑯᑲᓱᒡ, ᒥᒄ ᑭᒋᐧᑲᐋᐤ᙮ ᒥᒄ ᐅᐢᑎ:ᑲᓂᑲᒻ ᒥᐢᑎ:ᑲ ᐊᔭᐱᓴᐢᑯᓯᔪᒋ; ᓂᔭᔦᐋ ᐃᔭᐢᐱᑕᐢᑯᓯᔪᒋ ᒥᐢᑎ:ᑲ᙮ ᐅᑕ ᐋᒋ ᑭᒋᐧᑲᐋᐨ ᐊᐅᑯᓂ ᒐ ᐅᑭᐢᑯᑐᐋᐨ᙮ ᒻᒻᒻ᙮ ᒐᐋᐨ᙮

ᓂᐢ:ᑕᐢ:ᑲᐊᐤ ᐅᑭᐢ:ᑲ᙮

ᐊᑯ ᑕᐸᑲ ᐊᐢ:ᑕᑯᐤ ᓂ ᒥᒋᒥᔦᐤ ᐊᑲ ᐊᑕᒋ᙮ ᐊᑯ ᒪᒥᒋᓱᐨ ᑲ ᐱᒐᐨ᙮

ᐊᑯ ᑲ ᒥᒋᓱᒡ ᐃᑕᐤ, “ᓂᒥᐢ,” ᐃᑕᐤ, “ᓂᑐᐚᐱᒥᒡ ᒪ ᐊᓐᑕ,” ᐃᑕᐤ, “ᓂᐨ ᐊᒐᐱ,” ᐃᑕᐤ᙮ “ᓂᑭ ᒧᐧᑯᑕᐤ,” ᐃᑕᐤ᙮ ᑕᐸᑲ ᐅᑕᐚᐚ ᐅᒧᐧᑯᑕᑭᓂᔦᐤ ᑎᑯᓂᔦᐤ, ᑭᓄᐚᔨᑎ:ᒪᐅᒡ ᐃᔭᐱᒡ᙮

ᐊᑯ ᓇᑐᐚᐸᑕᐧᐠ᙮ ᐊᐅᑯᓂ ᐅᔭᔦᐚ ᐅᐨᐊᒐᐱᔭ ᒥᐟ ᐱᐱᒋᑲᐚᔨᐱᐣ ᒥᐢᑎ:ᑲ᙮ ᒼᒼᒼ᙮

“ᒋᐸᒋ ᐑ ᑐᑐᐚᐤ, ᓇᔨ; ᐊᑯ ᑕᐸᓂᑕ ᐃᔨᓇᑯᐚᑭᓄᐤ ᐊᒐᐱᐢ,” ᐃᑕᐤ᙮

“ᐊᑯ ᐸᓱ ᐊᑯᐢ, ᐸᓱ᙮”

ᐸᑎᑲᐊᔨᒋ᙮ ᐸᑕᔭᐢᑯᓂᒪᑯᐨ᙮ ᒪᒧᐧᑯᑕᐨ ᒐᐢᐊᐨ ᐅᐨᐊᒐᐱᔭ᙮ ᒥᐟ ᒪᒪᒥᐧᑯᑕᐤ; ᑕᐸᐑ ᒥᒥᔦᐧᑯᑕᐤ᙮

ᐊᑯ ᐃᑕᐤ, “ᐑᐑᑎᓯᓐ,” ᐃᑕᐤ᙮

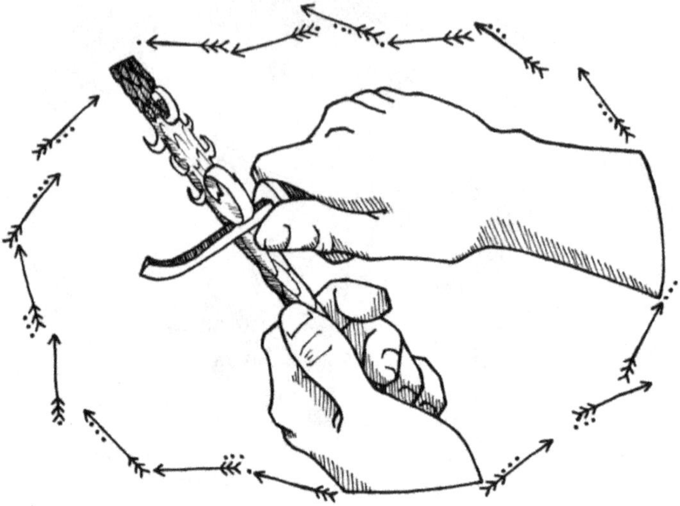

ᐋᔦᐧᐃᑎᓯᓇᔨᒥ᙮

“ᐸᒋ ᐱᑎᑲᐊᔨᒡ ᓂᑭᐢᑯᒡ,” ᐃᑕᐤ᙮ ᐸᑎᑲᐊᔨᒥ᙮

ᒪᒧᐧᑯᑕᑦ ᒥᓐ, ᑕᐸ ᐧᐃ ᒥᒥᔦᐧᑯᑕᐤ᙮ ᓇᐢᑎᐢ ᒥ ᐋᐋᑎᐧᑯᑕᐤ ᐅᑕ ᐅᐢᑎ:ᑲᓂᒪᒡ᙮ ᒥᒄ ᐅᑕ ᓱᓱᐋᐢᑯᐧᑯᑕᓱᐤ ᐊᓐᑕ ᐊ ᐱᒪᐢᑯᓯᓂᔨᒥ᙮ ᐊᑯᑕ ᐊᓐᑕ ᒥᒄ ᒧᐧᑯᑕᑦ, ᒋᒋᐋ ᑲᒋ ᓱᓱᐧᐃᐧᑯᑕᑦ :ᑲ ᐃᓯᓇ:ᑲᐊᑦ᙮ ᒻᒻᒻ᙮

•••

ᐊᐦᐊᒃ, ᐊᐦᐊᒃ; ᐊᐦᐊᒃ ᐊᑯ, “ᓂᒥᓴ, ᒐ ᐃᔭᔭᓐ᙮”

ᒐᒋᓴᐸᔭᔨᒡ ᐋᔦᐧᐃᑦ, ᐋᔦᐧᐃᑦ᙮

ᐋᔦᐧᐃᑦ ᑕᓐᑕ ᐋᐋᑕᔨᑕᐧᒃ ᑭᐹ ᐱᑎᒪ; ᐋᔦᐧᐃᑦ᙮

“ᓄᑕᐧᐃᔾ ᒪᓂᔭ ᑲ ᓂᐸᐃᑯᐋ:ᑲ ᐊᐋᔦᐋ, ᐊᑐᒡ ᑲᑭᔭ ᓂᒋ ᓂᑐᐋᐱᒪᐤ, ᓂᒋ ᓂᑐᐋᐱᒪᐤ,” ᐃᑕᔨᑎᒻ᙮

ᒐ ᐧᐃ ᑎᐸᐊᒧᐋᑦ ᐅᑕᐧᐃᔭ᙮ ᒻᒻᒻ᙮

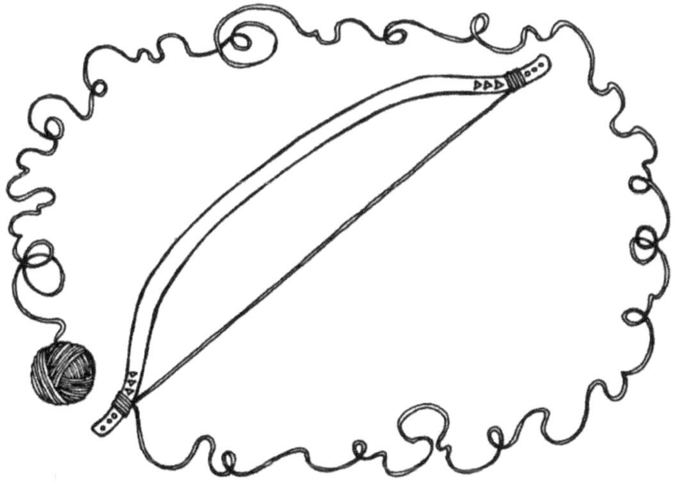

ᐊᐦᐊᕽ ᐸᒐᑦ᙮

“ᐸᑕ, ᓂᒥᓴ,” ᐃᑕᐤ, “ᒐ ᐅᑕᒐᐸᑐᔭᓐ,” ᐃᑕᐤ᙮

ᒪᔨᑯᑦ ᐊᐱᓯᓯᐤ᙮

ᐊᑯ ᐅᓴᓯᐚ ᐅᑎ ᓄᒋᐧᑯᐚ ᐅᑭᐢᐧᑳ ᐅᓴᓯᐚ, “ᓂᒥᓴ,” ᐃᑕᐤ, “ᒍᑕᐄᓄᐤ ᒪᓂᔭᐧᑲ,” ᐃᑕᐤ, “ᑕᓐ ᐊᓯᓇᑯᓯᔨᒋ ᐊᓂᔭ ᓇᐸᐃᑯᐠ ᐊᐚᓯᐚ?” ᐃᑕᐤ᙮

“ᓇᓯ,” ᐃᑎᑯᐤ, “ᐚᓴ ᒋᒋᐚ ᑯᐢᑕᑕᔨᑕᑯᓯᐤ; ᒥᓯᑐᐤ ᒋᒋᐚ,” ᐃᑎᑯᐤ᙮

“ᓂᐦᐃ,” ᐃᑕᐤ᙮

ᒥ ᒋᐢᑐᑕᐤ; ᒥ ᐄᑎᒧᐚᐤ ᒐ ᓂᑐᐚᐱᒪᑦ᙮

“ᓂᒥᓴ,” ᐃᑕᐤ, “ᓇᑕ ᒪ ᓂᑭ ᓇᓂᑐᐚᐱᒪᐅᐠ ᐊᓂᐢᑎᑯᒐᓯᐠ,” ᐃᑕᐤ᙮ “ᐅᑕ ᒥᑎᒪ ᓂᑭ ᐱᐸᒧᑕᓐ,” ᐃᑕᐤ᙮

“ᓂᐦᐃ,” ᐃᑎᑯᐤ᙮

• • •

ᐧᐃᐱᒡ ᑲᐊᑎ ᐦᑐᑕᑦ, ᓇᑐᐧᐋᐱᒪᑦ ᑲᒋᑐᐧᐋᐦ:ᑲ᙮

ᓂᔭᔪᐤ ᒪᒃ ᐊᓐᑕ ᓂᔭᑎ:ᒪᑦ ᐅᑕᐧᐃᔭ᙮ (ᑕᐸ ᐅᓇᓯᑎ:ᒪᐤ ᐊᓐᑕ ᑲ ᓂᐸᐃᑯᓯᒋ᙮)

ᓂᔭᑎ:ᒪᑦ᙮

ᐊᑯ ᐊᓐᑕ ᐊᓯᓂᔪᐤ ᐊᐦᑕᔪᐤ ᒥᒐᐱᐦᑲᔪᐤ᙮ ᐊᐅᑯᔪᐤ ᓂᔭᑕᐧᒃ᙮ ᐊᑯ ᓂᔭᔪᐧᐋ ᐅᑭᐦ:ᑲ ᑭᔭᔭᑦ ᓇᑕ, ᐧᐋᔪᐧᐃᐦ ᓇᑕ ᑭᔭ ᐅᑦᐊᒐᐱᔭ᙮ ᐊᓯᑯᓂᑲᐧᐋᑦ ᓇᑕ᙮ ᐊᑯ ᓂᔭᔪᐤ ᐊᓯᓂᔪᐤ ᓂᔭᑕᐧᒃ᙮ ᐊᑯ ᓇᑕ ᑕᐧᑯᒡ ᓇᑕ ᐊᑯᑕ ᐸᒥᓯᐧᒃ᙮ ᐸᒥᓯᓂᐦᑦ᙮

ᓇᑭᒧᐦᑦ:

“ᑲᒋᑐᐧᐋᐦᑯ ᓂᑐᓂᒐᐊᐤ,
ᑲᒋᑐᐧᐋᐦᑯ ᓂᑐᓂᒐᐊᐤ᙮”

• • •

“ᒪ! ᐊᐋᓐ ᐊᑯ? ᓂᑐᑐᐄ·ᒄ ᒪ ᐊ ᐃ:ᑕᐅᑦ᙮ ᓂᑐᐋᐱᒻ! ᑭᔅᔪᒄ, ᓂᑐᐋᐱᒻ! ᒥᔅᒄ, ᒥᔅᒄ ᓂᑐᐋᐱᒻ!”

ᓇᑐᐋᐱᒪᑦ ᒥᔅᒄ᙮ ᒻᒻᒻ᙮

ᐊᐅᑯᓂ ᐅᔪᔦᐋ ᐸᒥᓯᓂᕆᑭ ᐊᓯᓂᒡ᙮ ᒻᒻᒻ᙮ ᒐᑐᑎᑯᑦ,

“ᐊᐋ ᐅ ᑭᔾ ᖃᑭᑐᐋᔅᒄ ᐊᑎᑯᕆᓐ?”

“ᓇᒪ᙮” ᐃᑕᐤ, “ᓇᒪᔪᐤ ᓂᔾ᙮”

“ᐊᐦᐊᒃ, ᑭᐋᒪ ᐊᓐᑕ,” ᐃᑕᐤ᙮ “ᖃᑭᑐᐋᔅᒄ ᐊᐅᒄ,” ᐃᑕᐤ᙮ “ᐊᐅᒄ ᓇᑐᓂᒐᐊᒃ᙮”

ᑕᑯᓯ·ᒃ ᒥᔅᒄ᙮

“ᑕᓐ ᐊᑎᑦ?” ᐃᑕᐅᒡ᙮

“‘ᒥᔪᐤ ᑭᔾ ᓇᑐᐋᕆᒥᑕᓐ’ :ᑲ ᐃᓯᑦ,” ᐃᑕᐤ᙮ “‘ᖃᑭᑐᐋᔅᒃ ᐊᐅᑯᓐ ᓇᑐᐋᕆᒥᒃ’ :ᑲ ᐃᓯᑦ,” ᐃᑕᐤ᙮

“ᑭᔾ ᒪ, ᑭᔾ ᒪ, ᐋᐱᔅᒄ! ᓂᑐᐋᐱᒻ!”

ᓇᑐᐋᐱᒥᑯᑦ ᐋᐱᔅ:ᑲ᙮

ᐊᐅᑯᓂ ᐱᔪᑐᑕᕆᑭ, ᐄᐱᒡ ᐱᔪᑭ ᐸᓱᓇᑯᓯᕆᑭ, ᔅᔅ :ᑲ ᑭᑐᑕᑦ᙮

ᐃᑕᐤ, “ᐊᐋ ᑭᔾ ᖃᑭᑐᐋᔅᒄ?” ᐃᑕᐤ᙮

“ᓇᒪ,” ᐃᑎᑯᐤ᙮

“ᖃᑭᑐᐋᔅᒄ ᐊᐅᒄ ᓇᑐᓂᒐᐊᒃ,” ᐃᑎᑯᐤ᙮

ᒐᐋᕆᑭ᙮

ᑕᑯᓯᓂᔨᒋ, “ᑕᓐ ᐊᑎᑦ?” ᐃᑕᐅᒡ᙮

“‘ᑲᒋᑐᐋᔅᒄ ᐊᐅᒄ ᓇᑐᓂᒐᐊᒃ,’ ᑯᓴᑦ,” ᐃᑕᐤ᙮ “‘ᒋᐋᒪ,’ ᐊ:ᑲᓯᑦ,” ᐃᑕᐤ᙮ “ᓂ ᒋᐋᑎᓴᐅᒃ᙮”

ᐊᑯ ᐊᓐ ᑲᒋᑐᐋᔅᒄ, “ᑕᓐ ᐊᓯᓇᑯᓯᑦ ᐊᓐ?” ᐃᑕᐤ᙮

“ᒋᒋᐋ ᐊᐱᓯᔑᐤ,” ᐃᑕᐤ ᐋᐱᔅᒄ᙮ “ᐊᓯᓂᒡ ᐊᓐᑕ ᒋᔅᒋᓂᔑᐤ,” ᐃᑕᐤ᙮ “ᐊᐱᓯᔑᐤ ᒋᒋᐋ,” ᐃᑕᐤ᙮ “ᑭ ᐱᓴᐸᒋᐋᔑᐋ :ᑲ ᐃᓯᓇᑯᓯᑦ,” ᐃᑕᐤ᙮ “ᑭ ᒋᓇ̈ᐸᒋᔑᐋ :ᑲ ᐃᓯᓇᑯᓯᑦ,” ᐃᑕᐤ᙮

• • •

ᐊᑯ, “ᓂᑭ ᓂᑐᐋᐱᒪᐤ,” ᐃᑕᐤ ᑲᒋᑐᐋᔅᒄ᙮

ᐸᓯᑯᑦ᙮ ᒥᓯᑐᐤ ᑕᓐᑕ, ᑭ ᓇᓇᒥᐱᔦᐋ ᐊᔅᒋᔦᐤ ᐸᓯᑯᑦ᙮

ᒻᒻᒻ᙮ “ᐊᐅᒄ, ᐊᐅᒄ ᐊ·ᐃᒐ᙮” ᑕᐸ ᐅᓇᔨᒪᔑᐤ᙮

ᓂᓴᔦᐋ ᒥᔅᑎ:ᑲ ᓯᓴ:ᑲᔅᑯᓯᔨᒋ ᐊᐱᑐᐋᔅᒄ ᓇᑕ

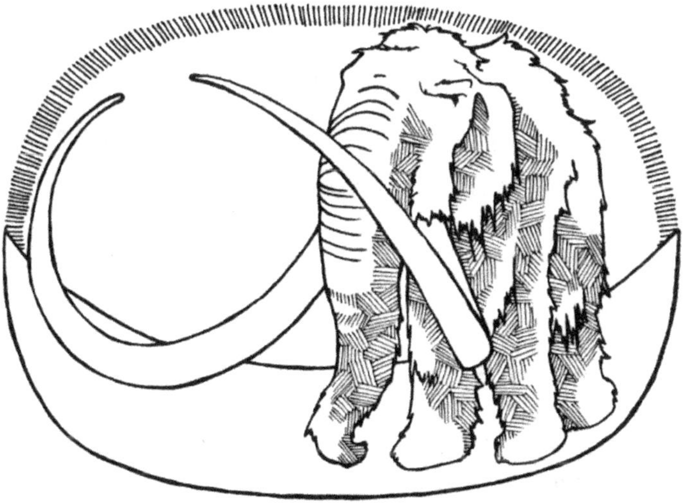

:ᑲ ᐃᔅᑎᑯᑕᔨᒡ ᐅᔅᑎ:ᑲᓂᔦᐤ, ᓯᔭ:ᑲᔅ:ᑲᐊᒥᔨᒋ'᙮

“ᐊᐅᑯᐄᒐ,” ᐃᑕᔨᒪᐤ᙮ ᒐᑐᔅᑐᐋᑦ, ᒐᑐᔅᑐᐋᑦ, ᑭ ᓂᐱᓱᐋ :ᑲ ᑎᑦ, ᒥ ᐊᒋᓱᐤ ᓇᔅᑎᔅ᙮ ᓂᔭᑕᑦ ᑲᒋᑐᐋᔅᒄ, ᐊᐅᑯᓂ ᐸᒥᓯᓂᓯᔨᒋ ᐊᓯᓂᒡ ᑕᐧᑯᒡ᙮

“ᓇᐊᐊ,” ᐃᑕᐤ, “ᐊᐋ ᑲᒋᑐᐋᔅ:ᑲ ᑲ ᓇᓂᑐᓂᒐᐊᑦ?” ᐃᑕᐤ᙮ “ᓇᔅᑎᔅ ᐅᐋ ᐊᑲ ᐊᔭᐱᒋᓇᑯᓱᐋ ᐊᑲ ᒋ ᐃᓯᓇᑯᓱᐋ,” ᐃᑕᐤ᙮

ᐋᒋ ᓂᑐᑕᑯᔅᑦ᙮

“ᐋᐋᒡ ᐅᔭ ᓴᔅ ᑭ ᓇᔅ:ᑕᔨᑎᒍᓯᐱᓄᐋ,” ᐃᑕᐤ᙮

“ᐅᑕ ᐋᒋ ᐅᑕᐋᑦ ᐅᔭ ᐅᔅᑐᓐ ᐅᔭ,” ᐃᑕᔨᒥᑯᐤ ᓇ ᐃᔭᐱᒡ᙮ “ᑭᒪ ᐋᐱᔅᑐᓇᒥᔨᓐ ᓇᑕ ᓂᑭᔅᑯᒡ ᐊᐱᒡ,” ᐃᑕᔨᒥᑯᐤ᙮ ᐋᔦᐄᔅ ᓇᑕ ᐊᐱᔦᐋ ᐅᑭᔅ:ᑲ᙮

ᐄᔭᐱᔅᑐᓇᒪᑦ ᐅᔭᔦᐋ ᐅᔅᑐᓐ ᐋᒋ ᐋᐱᔅᑯᐋᑦ᙮ ᓇᑕ ᓇᐊᐤ ᐅᑭᔅᑯᔦᐋ ᐊᐱᔨᒋ, ᐊᑯᑕ ᓇᑕ ᐱᔭᔅᒋᓂᔨᒋ;

:ᑲ ᒋᓂᔅᑎᐱᑲᐳᓯᔑᒋ᙮

“ᑕᓐᑕ ᐅ ᓂᔭᔅ:ᑕᔑᑎᒥᔑᒋ,” ᐃᑎᑯᐤ᙮

ᑭ ᒋᑕᐱᒪᐋ ᑲᒋᑐᐋᔅᒄ᙮ ᒧᔅᒋᐧᑯᓂᒋᓇᔑᒋ ᐅᑭᔅᑯᔦᐋ ᑭᔭ ᐅᑦ ᐊᒐᐱᔦᐋ᙮ ᑲ ᒧᔅᒋᐧᑯᓂᒋᓇᔑᒋ, ᒐᑐᑎᑯᑦ, “ᓄᑕᐧᐃᔾ ᒪ ᑲ ᓂᐸᐃᑯᐋ:ᑲ ᑕᓐ ᐊᔅᐱᔅ ᒥᔅᑯᓯᔑᒋ,” ᐃᑕᐤ᙮

• • •

ᐊ :ᑕᒧᐋᑦ ᐋᒋᓇᑭᓇᑎ:ᑲ ᒋᒥᓱᔦᐋ, ᒥᓯᑎᒋᓱ:ᔭ᙮

ᐋᑕᒋᔅᑐᐋᔑᒋ ᐸ:ᒪᔑᒋ᙮ ᓇᐦᐊᐤ ᒥᓯᐋᐤ ᓂᔭᔦᐋ ᐋᒋᓇᑭᓇᑎ:ᑲ :ᑲ ᐱᓯᑎᑲᐋᑦ᙮

“ᑕᐸ ᐃᔅᐱᔅ ᒥᔅᑯᓯᔦᐋ, ᒥ ᐃᔅᐱᔅ ᒥᔅᑯᓯᔦᐋ,” ᐃᑕᐤ ᑲᒋᑐᐋᔅᒄ᙮

ᐊᑯ ᐅᑕ ᐸᒋᓄᐋᑲᐱᔅᑲᔦᐤ ᐊᓯᓂᔦᐤ, ᐊᓯᓂᔦᐤ ᐱᔅᑯᑎᓇᐤ ᐅᑕ ᐃᓯᓇᑯᓂᔦᐋ, ᐅᑕ ᐊᓯᓂᔦᐤ ᐊᔅᑕᔑᒃ᙮

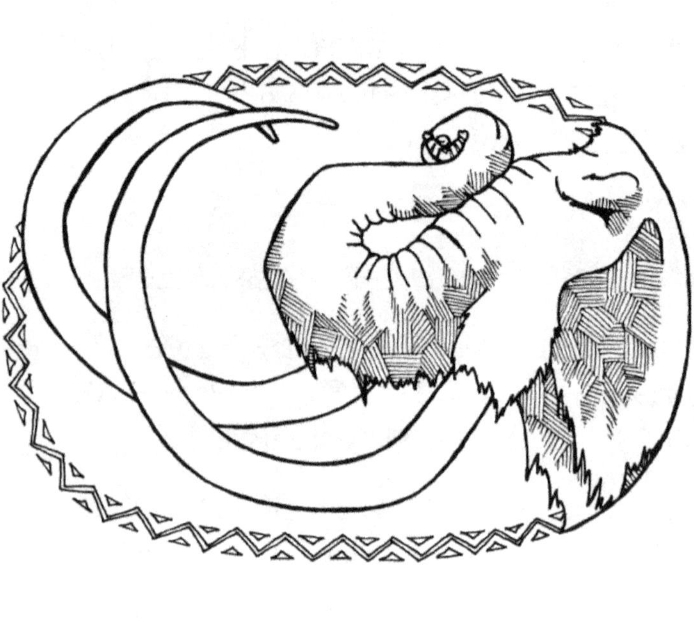

“ᒪᐤ ᖃ ᐃᔅᐱᔅ ᒥᔅᑯᓯᔨᒋ,” ᐃᑕᐤ, “ᓂᔭᔦᐋ ᐊ ᒋᔅᒐᑲᔨᒡ᙮”

ᐋᑎᓇᔨᒋ ᐅᑭᔅᑯᔦᐋ᙮ ᐸᒍᑎᒥᔨᒋ ᖃ ᓂᑭᔅᑲᐊᒥᔨᒋ᙮

ᖃᔅᑕᑦ, ᐊᐅᑯᔦᐤ ᖃᔅᑕᑦ᙮

ᐊᑎ ᒋᐋᔦᐋᐱᔦᐅᑦ, ᑕᓐᑕ ᐸᐃᒃ ᐃᔅᑯᓇᔦᐋ ᐅᑭᔅᑯᔦᐋ᙮ ᐸᒍᑯᑦ ᐊᑎ ᒋᐋᔦᐋᐱᔦᐅᑦ ᓇᐅᑕ ᒥᓱᑯᐤ᙮ ᖃ ᐱᑯᓱᑯᓇᐅᑯᑦ ᐊᓂᔭ ᐊᑕᐅᑯᑦ᙮ ᐸᐸᒥᑕᒋᒥᐸᑕᑦ ᑲᒋᑐᐋᔅᒃ᙮

ᓂᔭᑕᔨᒋ ᐅᑭᔅᑯᔦᐋ, ᐅᔭᔦᐋ ᑲ ᐱᒍᒐᔨᒋ, ᐋᑎᓇᔨᒋ ᓂᔭᑎᑯᑦ ᒥᓐ ᖃᔅᑕᒐ ᐋᒋ ᐱᒍᑯᑦ᙮

“ᓂ"ᐃ ᑕᐹ,” ᐃᑕᐤ, “ᑕᐹ ᒋ ᓂᐸᐃᓐ,” ᐃᑕᐤ ᑲᒋᑐᐋᔅᒃ᙮ ᐃᔨᒥᐃᑯᐤ ᑕᓐᑕ᙮ “ᒋ ᓂᐸᐃᓐ ᑕᐹ᙮ ᒻᒻᒻ᙮ ᐊᑯ ᒪᐤ ᒐ ᑐᑐᐧᐃᔨᓐ: ᒐ ᐱᑯᓱᐧᐃᔨᓐ᙮ ᐊᑯ ᐅᔭᔦᐋ ᓂᑐᑭᔭ ᐅᔭᔦᐋ ᐊᐅᑯᓂ ᒐ ᒥᓂᓯᒥᓐ,” ᐃᑕᐤ᙮ “ᐊᐅᑯᓂ ᐅᔭᔦᐋ

ᒐ ᐊᐱᒋᑕᔨᓐ," ᐃᑕᐤ᙮

ᒼᒼᒼ᙮ "ᓂᐦᐃ," ᐃᑎᑯᐤ᙮

•••

ᐸᐱᑯ:ᓯᑦ᙮ ᐊᑯ ᐅᔭᔦᐋ ᐄᑐᑲᔦᐋ ᐅᔭᔦᐋ ᐊᐅᑯᓂ ᐅᔭᔦᐋ ᒥᔭᐋᔨᑎ:ᒪᑦ᙮ ᒪᓂᓯ:ᒪᑦ, ᓇ:ᓯᐱᐧᑲᑕᐧᐠ; ᐄᑐᑲᒪ ᓇ:ᓯᐱᐧᑲᑕᐧᐠ᙮

ᐊᑯ ᒐᐋᑐᐅᑕᑦ᙮

ᐊᑯ ᐅᑕ ᐱᔭᒋ ᐱᐢᑐᐅᑕᑦ ᒋᐱᐢ:ᑲᒡ ᐸᒐᑦ᙮

ᐊᑯ ᒪᒥᒋᓱᑦ, ᑭᔦ ᐅᒥᓯ ᒪᔨᑯᑦ ᒥᒋᒥᔦᐤ᙮ ᐊᑯ ᐅᔭ ᐅᑎ ᒥᒋᓱ, "ᓂᒥᓯ," ᐃᑕᐤ, "ᐊᓐᑕ ᒪ ᓂ ᐸᑕᓐ ᒐ:ᑲᓂᒐᓂ, ᐱᑎᑭᑕ," ᐃᑕᐤ᙮

"ᒐ ᓄᒋᐧᑭᒥᓐ," ᐃᑕᐤ᙮

ᐸᓯᑯᓯᐸᑕᔨᒋ ᐅᒥᓯ ᓇᑐᐋᐸᑎᒥᔨᒋ ᐊᐅᑯᓂ ᐊᐢᑕᔨᒋ᙮ ᐅᐱ:ᔭᐄᔦᐋ ᒐ:ᑲᓂᔦᐋ ᒥᓯᔦᐋ; ᐊ ᓯᐱᐄᔨᒋ :ᑲᐢᑎᒥᔨᒋ᙮

"ᓇᓯ," ᐃᑎᑯᐤ, "ᒐ:ᑲᔦᐋ ᐅᔭᔦᐋ?" ᐃᑎᑯᐤ᙮

"ᒍᑕᐄᓄᐤ ᑲ ᓂᐸᐃᑯᐋ:ᑲ ᐊᐋᔦᐋ: ᓂᔭᔦᐋ ᐄᑐᑭᔦᐋ ᐊᐅᑯᓂ ᓂᔭᔦᐋ," ᐃᑕᐤ᙮ "ᓂ ᓂᐸᐃᒪᐋ," ᐃᑕᐤ᙮ "ᐱᑎᑭᑕ," ᐃᑕᐤ, "ᒐ ᓄᒋᐧᑭᒥᓐ," ᐃᑕᐤ᙮ "ᒐ ᐅᓂᐸᑭᓂᐧᑯᔨᓐ, ᑭᔭ ᓂᐢᑦ ᐸᐃᐠ ᒐ ᐅᓂᐸᑭᓂᔨᓐ᙮" ᑕᓐᑕ ᒥᓯᔦᑲᔦᐋ᙮

ᐸᑎᑭᑕᔨᒋ ᐊ ᐃᑎᓱᒪᑦ ᐊ ᐃᑎᔨᒋ᙮ ᐊᑯ ᓄᒋᐧᑭᒥᔨᒋ, ᐊᔦᑯᓂ ᐋᓂᐸᑭᓂᐧᑲᑯᑦ᙮

2. ᒐᐧᑲᐸᐢ ᑭᓭ ᑳᐚᐚᐱᓱᐚᐊᒃ ᐊᐚᔦᐚ

ᑭᓭᑭᓴᐸᓭᔨᐠ ᐚᓂᑦ᙮

ᐱᓭᑐᐚᑦ; ᐱᓭᑐᐚᑦ ᐊᓐᑕ ᐊᐚᔦᐚ ᐊᓐᑕ ᐊᑕᐧᐃᔨᒋ᙮ ᒻᒻᒻ᙮ “ᓂᒥᓴ, ᐊᐚᒐᓂᒋ ᒪᓐᑕ ᑭ ᒥᑐᐚᐚᐱᓱᑎᑭᒋ?”

“ᓇᓯ, ᐊᑲ ᓂᑐᐚᐱᒥᒃ; ᐚᓴ ᐊᓐᒃ ᒋᒋᐚ ᒥ ᐃᐹᐧᑲᐅᒃ᙮ ᐅᑎᑎ:ᑕᐚ, ᐊᑯ ᒐ ᐚᐚᐱᓱᓂᐢᒃ᙮

ᐊᑯ ᑯᑐᐚᐅᒃ, ᐊᓐᑕ ᐊᑯᑕ ᓇᑕ ᐊᐢᑕᒃ ᐅᑦ ᐊᐢᒋᐧᑯᐚᐤ, ᒥᓴᔦᐤ᙮ ᐊᑯ ᐧᐃᓭᐚᐱᓱᓇ:ᑕᐧᐃ ᐃᔦᐚ, ᓂᓭᔦᐚ ᐊᐢᐱᔨᒋ ᓂᓭᔦᐚ, ᐊᑯ ᐸᐢᑲᐸᓯ:ᒪᒃ ᓂᓭᔦᐚ, ᓂᓭᔦᐚ ᐊᐱᓯᔦᐚ᙮ ᐊᑯ ᓂᓭᔦᐚ ᐅᑦ ᐊᐢᒋᐧᑯᐚᐤ, ᓂᓭᔦᐚ ᐊᑯᑕ ᓇᑕ ᐳᑕᑭᒥᐱᔨᒋ᙮ ᐊᑯ ᐊᐢ:ᑲᓱᔨᒋ ᐅᑕᔦᐤ ᓂᓭᔦᐚ ᐅᑦ ᐊᐢᒋᐧᑯᐚᐤ ᓇᐸᐃᑭᓱᔨᒋ᙮”

“ᓂᐦᐃ ᓂᒥᓴ, ᒥᓂᑭ ᒋ ᓂᑐᐚᐱᒪᐅᒃ᙮ ᒋ ᑯᐢᑕᒋᒥᓐ ᐅᓴᒻ ᐊ ᐃᑕᒋᒍᔨᓐ,” ᐃᑕᐤ᙮

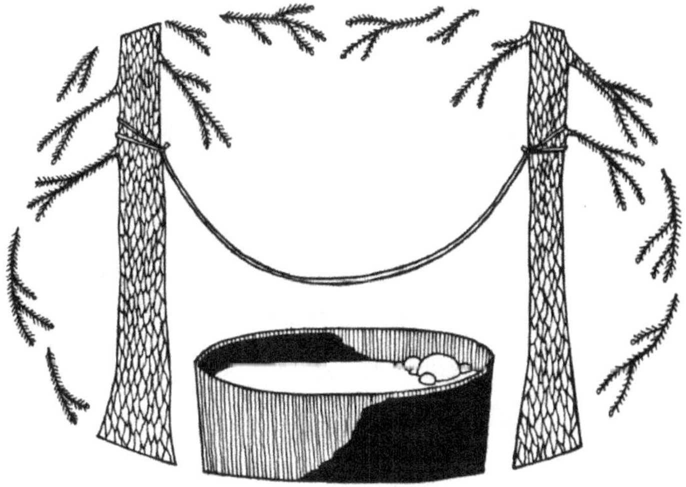

• • •

ᐄᐱᒡ ᑲ ᐋᑕᔅᐱᓱᑦ, ᓇᑐᐋᐱᒪᑦ᙮

ᐊᐅᑯᐤ ᐋᒋ ᓴᑲᔅ:ᑲᔅᑦ, ᒥᓯᑎᔦᐋ ᐅᑦᓴᒪ ᑭᔭ ᐅᑦ ᐊᒐᐱᔭ ᒥᓯᑎᔦᐋ, ᑭ ᐊᐱᓯᓯᓱᐋ :ᑲ ᐃᓯᓇᑯᓯᑦ᙮

“ᒪ! ᒪᓐᑕᐤ ᐋᑎᑕᐧᒄ᙮ ᐋᐋᐱᓱᓂᐃᒄ!” ᑲ ᐃᑎᑯᑦ ᐅᒥᓴ᙮ ᒻᒻᒻ᙮

“ᐋᐋᐱᓱ ᒪᓐᑕᐤ!”

ᐋᐸᑎ:ᒪᐤ ᐅᑦ ᐊᔅᒋᑯᔦᐤ ᐊᔅᑕᔑᒡ᙮

ᐊᐦᐊᒃ, ᒐᒥᔭᑦ ᓇᑕ ᐅᑭᔅ:ᑲ, ᓂᔅᑎᔦᐋ ᐅᑭᔅ:ᑲ; ᒐᒥᔭᔅᑦ ᓇᑕ᙮ ᐊᑯ ᐅᔭᔦᐋ ᐅᑦ ᐊᒐᐱᔭ, ᐅᔭᔦᐋ ᐅᔭᔦᐤ ᐅᑦ ᐊᒐᐸᔅ:ᑲ, ᐊᐅᑯᓂ ᒥ ᐱᔅᑎᓇᐤ᙮ ᐊᑯ ᓂᔭᔦᐤ ᒐ ᐸᒋ ᒋᑐᑕᑦ ᓂᔭᔦᐤ, ᒋ ᐅᓯᑕᔦᐋ ᑐᒥ:ᑲᓇ ᐅᒥᓴ, ᒋ ᑭᓄᐋᔑᑎᒥᔦᐋ᙮ ᐊᐅᑯᓂ ᑲ ᒐᒍᑎᒪᑦ ᐱᔭᐱᑕᐊᐧᒃ ᐅᑕ ᐅᑕ ᐅᑎᐧᑯᒡ; ᓂᔭᔦᐤ ᑐᒥ:ᑲᓇ, ᐊ ᓂᓯᓂᔑᒋ᙮

ᐊᑯ ᐅᑕ ᐊᑎᑕᐧᒃ ᐅᑕ ᐅᑎᐧᑯᒡ ᒐ ᐱ:ᑲᑕᐅᑦ ᐅᑕ, ᒐ ᐊᑲ ᒋ ᐸᒋᑕᑦ᙮ ᒻᒻᒻ᙮

ᐋᐋᑎᐱᑦ ᒋᑭᓴᒻ᙮ (ᒥ ᒥᓇᐤ ᐅᑦ ᐊᓴᒪ, ᑭᔭ ᐅᑦ ᐊᒐᐸᔅ:ᑲ ᑕᐧᑯᓇᐤ᙮)

• • •

ᐊᑯ ᐃᑕᐤ, “ᐋᔅ ᒪᓐ ᒐ ᐃᑐᑐᔭᒄ,” ᐃᑕᐤ, “ᒪᐊᓐ ᐊᒄ ᒋᑦ ᐊᔅᒋᐧᑯᐋᐤ,” ᐃᑕᐤ, “ᒐᔅᑎᓇᔅ ᐊᑯᑕ ᓇᑕ ᒐ ᐸᒋᓯᓂᔭᓐ ᒐ ᐱᔅᑲᐸᓱᔭᒄ,” ᐃᑕᐤ᙮ “ᐊᑯ ᓇᑕ ᐸᒋᓯᓂᔭᓇ,” ᐃᑕᐤ, “ᐱᒥᓱᔭᓇ ᒪᒃ,” ᐃᑕᐤ᙮ “ᐊᑯ ᒐ ᐋᔅᑲᐱᔅᑐᔭᒄ, ᒐ,” ᐃᑕᐤ᙮ “ᒐ ᓄᑕᐳᐋᓯᔭᒄ,” ᐃᑕᐤ,

“ᐊ ᐱᒥᓱᔭᓐ,” ᐃᑕᐤ, “ᓂᑭ ᐱᒥᓱᓐ ᒋᒋᐋ᙮” ᐃᑕᐤ᙮

ᐧᐃᔭᐋᐱᒐᓂᑯᑦ, ᑭᐹ ᒐᓯᐱᔑᑦ ᐊ ᐃᔅᐱᔑᑦ ᐅᔭᔦᐤ᙮

ᐊᑯ ᓂᔭᔦᐤ ᐸᐃᒄ, ᓂᔭᔦᐤ ᐊᐱᓯᔦᐤ, ᐋᑕᐸᑭᒧᔑᒡ ᓂᔭᔦᐤ, ᐋᑕᐸᑭᒧᔑᒡ ᐅᐱᔅ᙮ ᐸᓯᒥᔑᒋ ᐅᔭᔦᐤ ᐊᐱᓯᔦᐤ ᓇᐊᒻ ᐅᔭᔦᐋ ᐊᓂᔭ ᐅᑦ ᐊᔅᒋᐧᑯᔦᐤ, ᐊᑯᑕ ᓇᐊᒻ ᐱᔭᒋᓯᓂᔅᑦ᙮ ᒻᒻᒻ᙮

ᐊᑯᑕ ᓇᑕ ᒐ ᒧᔅᑲᒧᔅᑲᒍᓱᔅᑦ᙮ ᑕᐸ ᓂᐳᐤ, ᒥᒄ ᐅᒋ ᐃᑕᐱᒪᓱᐤ ᓇᑕ, ᐋᒋ ᓇᓇᑭᒐᐊᑦ᙮

ᑲ ᐃᑎᓱᒥᑕᐧᒄ, “ᐋᔅᑲᐱᔅᑐᒄ!” ᐧᐃᔭᔅᑲᐱᔅᑕᑯᒡ᙮ ᐊᑯ ᒥᓯᐋ ᑭ ᓇᑎᑯᒋ ᐊᑕᔑᒪᑦ ᑲ ᐋᔅᑲᐱᔅᑕᑯᒡ, ᑭᐹ ᒐ ᑭᓄᐋᐱᒪᑦ᙮

ᐃᔭᔭᒋᐱᔑᑕᐋᑦ ᓂᔭᔦᐤ ᐅᑦ ᐊᔅᒋᐧᑯᔦᐤ, ᐧᐃᔭᐅ:ᓴᐸᑲᒧᐋᑦ ᐅᔭᔦᐋ ᐅᑦ ᐊᒐᐸᔅ:ᑲ᙮ ᒥᓯᐋ ᐃᔅ:ᑲ:ᓴᐤ ᐅᑕ ᐅᔭᔑᒡ; ᒪᒪᔅᐱᓇᔑᒋ, ᐃᔭᓯ:ᑲᔑᒋ᙮

ᑕᓐᑕ ᒥᓯᐚ ᐃᐢ:ᑲ:ᓴᐤ; ᑭᔭ ᐅᑕ ᐅᐢᒋᓯᑯᐲᐠ ᒥᓯᐚ ᐃᐢ:ᑲ:ᓴᐤ᙮ ᐊᑯ ᐛᑎᑕᒥᐢᑎ:ᑲᓇᐛᐟ ᐅᐟ ᐊᒐᐸᐢ:ᑲ᙮

ᐊᑯ ᒥᓯᐚ ᓇᐸᐊᐟ᙮

“ᐅᓴ ᐅᐠ,” ᐃᑕᐤ, “ᓂ ᐏ ᒪᔭᔨᒥᑯᐠ,” ᐃᑕᐤ᙮ “ᑭ ᓂ ᐏ ᐱᐱᑲᐃᑯᐅᒋ ᐅᐟ ᐊᐢᒋᐧᑯᐚᐠ,” ᐃᑕᐤ᙮

ᓂᑭᑕᐤ, ᒐᐚᐟ᙮

ᑕᑯᓯᐧᒃ, ᒥ ᐏᑎᒧᐚᐤ ᐅᒥᓴ᙮

3. ᒐᐧᑲᐸᐦ ᑭᔭ ᐊᒐᓂᐦ:ᑲᐤ

ᐊᑯ ᒥᓐ ᐧᐃᔭᐱᓂᔩᒡ, "ᓂᒥᓴ ᐊᓐᑕ ᒪ ᐊᐙᓐᒋ ᑭ ᒥ:ᑕᐙᐦ:ᑲᐃᒐᑎᑭᒋ, ᑭ ᐱᐦ:ᑲᐃᒐᑎᑭᒋ?"

"ᐊᑲ ᓇᓯᒡ, ᓇᓯ᙮"

"ᒥᒋᓯᔪᐙ ᐊᓐᒡ ᐅᑳᐧᐃᐙ, ᒋᑭ ᓂᐸᐃᑯᔪᐙ; ᓂᐸᐊᔪᐙ ᐃᔪᐙ," ᐃᑎᑯᐤ᙮

ᐊᒐᓂᐦ:ᑲᐤ, ᐊᒐᓂᐦ:ᑲᐤ ᐃᓯᓂᑲᓱᔪᐙ᙮"

"ᐊᑯ ᐊᓐᒡ ᐃᐦ:ᑲᐅᒡ, ᓂᓱᒡ ᐊᓐᒡ, ᒋᔭᓅᐤ ᐊᑕᔫᑕᑯᓱᐙᐧᑯ, :ᑲ ᐃᑕᔫᑕᑯᓯᒡ ᐊᑎ:ᑲ ᐊᓐᒡ ᒧᐙᐅᒡ," ᐃᑎᑯᐤ᙮ "ᐃᓯ ᒥᒋᓱᐅᒡ, ᐃᓯ ᓂᑐᐧᐃᓱᐅᒡ," ᐃᑎᑯᐤ᙮

"ᐊᑯ ᓂᔭᔪᐙ ᐅᑳᐧᐃᐙ, ᐃᔪᐙ ᓂᔭᔪᐙ :ᑲ ᐃᓯ ᓂᑐᐧᐃᓱᔩᒋ᙮" ᐃᑎᑯᐤ᙮ ᒻᒻᒻ᙮ "ᒪᓴᐊᔪᐙ ᓂ ᐅᑳᐧᐃᐙ," ᐃᑎᑯᐤ᙮ "ᓇᑕ ᐃᓴᑯᔪᐤ ᐊᓐᑕ ᐧᐃ ᒋᒥᑕᔪᐙ ᐊᓐᑕ ᐊᐢᒋᒡ᙮ ᐊᑯᑕ ᐊᓐᑕ ᐧᐃᔭᐱᓇᔩᒋ ᓂ ᒥᔭᓴᐊᔩᒋ

ᐅᑲᐐᐙ," ᐃᑎᑯᐤ᙮ "ᐊᑯ ᓯᔭᐺᐢᑯᓯᒥᑯᔑᒋ ᐊᑯ ᓇᐸᔑᒋ ᓂ᙮"

"ᓂᒥᔅ, ᒥ ᓂᒋ ᓂᑐᐙᐱᒪᐅᐠ᙮ ᒋ ᑯᐢᑕᒋᒥᓐ ᐊ ᐃᑕᒋᒥᑦ," ᐃᑕᐤ᙮

• • •

ᐊᑯ ᑲ ᐚᑕᐢᐱᓱᐢᑦ᙮ ᐊᑯᑕ᙮

ᐃᑕᐤ, "ᓂᒥᔅ," ᐃᑕᐤ, "ᒥᒋᒪ ᐅᑕ ᓂᑭ ᐱᐸᒧᑕᓐ," ᐃᑕᐤ᙮ "ᐊᓂᐢᒋᑯᒐᓯᒡ ᓂᑭ ᓄᒋᐧᑯᐚᐅᒡ," ᐃᑕᐤ᙮ ᑕᐸ ᐐ ᐐᑎᒧᐙᐤ ᓂᔭᔪᐤ ᐚ ᐃᑎᑦ᙮

ᐐᐱᒡ ᓇᑕ ᑲ ᐊᑎ ᐊᑯᐢᐚᑯᓯᐧᒃ, ᓂᑐᐚᐱᒪᐤ ᓇᑕ ᑲ ᐸᑐᐚᑦ ᑲ ᑕᔑᒋ᙮

ᐊᐅᑯᐤ ᓯᔭ:ᑲᐢ:ᑲᐊᐧᐠ, ᐱᐢ:ᑲᐃᒐᐅᒡ ᐊᓇᒡ ᐃᐢ:ᑲᐅᒡ᙮ ᒼᒼᒼ᙮ “ᒪᐣᑕᐤ ᐚᑎᑕᐧᑯ,” ᐃᑕᐤ ᐅᓯᒪ᙮ ᓂᔭᑕᐟ ᐅᑕ ᐚᒋᑲᐳᐢᑐᐚᐟ᙮ ᐚᓱᓯᓄᐚᒡ, ᒍᒋᐃᑯᒡ ᐊᓇᒡ ᐃᐢ:ᑲᓯᒡ᙮ ᒼᒼᒼ᙮

• • •

ᐊᑯ ᐅᐚ ᐱᑎᑭᒥᒡ ᐅᑕ ᑕᐤ ᐅᐚ ᐊᒐᓂᐢ:ᑲᐤ ᐊᓯᓂᐧᑲᑕᑭᓄᐅᐟ᙮

“ᓂᑕᓂᐢ, ᒐ:ᑲᐣ ᑭ ᒧᓯᓇᓇᐚ?”

“ᐧᐃᐢᑭᒐᐣ ᐊᐣ ᓄᓯᓄᐚᓇᐣ ᓄᒋᐧᑭᒼ ᐅᐱᐧᐃᔭ,” ᐃᑎᑯᐤ᙮ ᐱᔭᐳᐧᐃᔨᒋ ᐊᐣᑕ᙮ ᓯᔭᒋᐚᐱᒪᐟ, ᓇᑐᐚᐱᒪᐟ᙮

ᐊᐅᑯᓂ ᐅᔭᔨᐚ᙮

ᓯᔭᒋᐚᐱᒪᐟ ᐊᐅᑯᐤ ᓇᐳᐧᐃᔨᒋ᙮ ᒼᒼᒼ᙮

“ᓂᑕᓂᐢ, ᓇᐸᒋᑭᐢᑯ ᐊ ᐊᐣ?”

"ᓇᐸᒋᑭᐢᐠ ᐊ?" ᐃᑎᑯᐤ᙮ "ᐊᑲ ᐸᒋ ᐃᔑᒧᐋᐊᑯ," ᐃᑎᑯᐤ ᐅᑕᓂᓴ᙮ ᒥ ᒋᐢᑐᐤ᙮ :ᑲ ᐃᓯᑲᐳᐑᔑᒋ᙮

ᐊᑯ ᐃᑎᑯᐤ, "ᓚᐢᑎᓇᐢ ᒋᑭ ᓂᐸᐃᐠ ᓂᑲᐑᓇᐣ; ᓂᐸᐊᐤ ᓂ ᐊᐋᔭᐋ ᐊᑎ ᐅᑎᓯᒥᔑᒋ ᓇᐸᐋ," ᐃᑎᑯᐤ᙮

"ᓂᐦᐃ," ᐃᑕᐤ᙮

"ᓂᑕᓂᐢ, ᐱᓚᐧᐠ ᐊᑯ, ᐱᓚᐧᐠ᙮"

ᒥ ᐑ ᐱᓚᔭᐋ ᐅᑕᓂᓴ᙮ ᒼᒼᒼ᙮ ᐊᑯ ᓚᒃ, ᐊᑯ ᐃᑕᐤ ᐊᐣ ᓚᐧᑲᐸᐢ, "ᐱᓚᐋᐧᐠ," ᐃᑕᐤ᙮ "ᓂᑭ ᐱᓚᐋᐣ ᐱᓚᐋ:ᑲ," ᐃᑕᐤ᙮ ᐊᑯ ᐸᓚᔑᒋ᙮ ᑲ ᐱᓚᔑ:ᑕᐤ ᐅᑕᓂᓴ, ᐊᑯ ᐸᓚᐟ ᓚᐧᑲᐸᐢ᙮

ᐊᑯ ᐊᐣᑕ ᐊᐱᐟ, ᐋᑎᐱᒪᐟ ᐅᓴᔭᐋ ᐃᐢ:ᑲᓴ᙮

ᐊᑯ, ᒼᒼᒼ, "ᓚ ᐊᓯᒥᒃ ᒪᐣᑕᐤ᙮"

ᐊᑯ ᓂᓴᔭᐋ ᐃᔭᐋ ᑲ ᒧᐋᐟ, ᐊᐅᑯᔭᐋ ᐋ ᐃᑎᓯᒪᐟ ᓂᐢᑎᒼ, ᐊᐅᑯᔭᐋ ᐋ ᐊᓯᒪᐟ!

ᑕᓐᑕ ᒋᐢᒐᔑᒪᐤ ᒐᐧᑲᐸᐢ ᓂᑎᒥᒄ ᐊ ᐃᓯ ᒥᒋᓱᔑᒋ᙮ ᒥ ᐧᐃ ᐅᑎᓂ:ᒪᐤ ᓂᔭᔦᐋ ᐊᓯᒥᑯᑦ, ᐱᒥᔦᐤ ᐊᓯᒥᑯᐤ; ᒥ ᐅᑎᓂ:ᒪᐤ, ᐊᓐᑕ ᐊᐢᑕᔑᒡ᙮

ᐊᑯ ᐅᒡ ᐃᐢ:ᑲᐅᒡ ᒪᔭᒡ ᐅᔭᔦᐋ ᒥᒋᒥᔦᐤ ᐊᓯ ᒥᒋᓱᒡ, ᐊᐅᑯᔦᐋ ᒪᒋᔑᒋ᙮ ᐊᓐ ᒐᐧᑲᐸᐢ ᐊᓯ ᒥᒋᓱᑦ᙮

• • •

ᐊᐅ:ᑲᓇ ᐋᔦᐧᐃᑦ ᐊᒐᓂᐢ:ᑲᐤ᙮

ᐊᐅᑯᓂ ᐅᔭᔦᐋ ᐅᑦ ᐊᒐᐱᔦᐋ ᒐᒥᔭᔑᒋ᙮ ᐋᑎᓂ:ᒪᑦ :ᑲ ᐊᑎ ᑯᑎᓂ:ᒪᑦ᙮ ᒻᒻᒻ᙮ "ᐱᒥᒋᑭᐢᑕᐤ, ᐱᒥᒋᑭᐢᑕᐤ᙮" ᒥ ᓱᓂᒪᐤ ᐅᑦ ᐊᒐᐱᔦᐋ ᐊᑎ ᑯᑎᓂ:ᒪᑦ, ᒐᒥᔑᒪᑦ᙮

"ᓂᑕᓂᐢ, ᒋᑭ ᐸᑐᑕᐤ ᒪ ᐊᑯ ᐊᓐᑕ ᐃᔦᐤ ᓂᑭ ᑯᑎᓂᒄ᙮"

"ᐊᑲ ᐧᐃᐧᐃ!" ᐋ ᐧᐃᐧᐃᐋᑦ ᒐᐧᑲᐸᐢ ᐊᓐᑕ, ᒪᒪᒋᑯᓂᑯᑦ᙮ "ᐊᑲ ᐧᐃᐧᐃ! ᐊᑲ ᓇᐢ!" ᐃᑎᑯᐤ᙮

"ᒪ ᐊᑲ ᑐᑐᐅᒄ᙮ ᓂᑭ ᓂᑐᐋᐱᒪᐤ," ᐃᑕᐤ᙮ "ᒐ ᐧᐃᐧᐃᐋᒄ, ᒥᓯᐋ ᒐ ᐧᐃᐧᐃᐋᒄ᙮"

"ᓂ"ᐃ," ᐃᑎᑯᐤ᙮

ᐋᔦᐧᐃᒡ, ᓇᑐᐋᐱᒪᒡ᙮

"ᐊ"ᐊᒃ, ᓂᑕᓂᐢ! ᒐ ᑯᑎᓂᒃ ᐃᔦᐤ!"

ᑲ ᐃᑕᒋᒪᑭᓄᐅᑦ ᐃᑕᔑᒪᐤ, ᒐᐧᑲᐸᐢ᙮ ᐊᑯ ᐋᐋᑎᓇᑦ, ᒥᔭᓯᐃᑯᑦ᙮

ᐊᑯ ᓂᔭᔦᐤ ᐃᐢᑯᔦᐤ ᓂᔭ ᑲ ᒋᒥᑕᑦ ᓇᑕ, ᒋᒥᑕᐤ ᓇᑕ ᐃᐢᑯᔦᐤ᙮ "ᐊᑯᑕ ᐊᓐᑕ ᒐ ᐋᐱᓂᒃ," ᐃᑕᔑᒪᐤ᙮ ᐊᑯᑕ

ᐊᓐᑕ ᐊᑎ ᐃᐢᐱᑕᑦx ᒐᐧᑲᐸᐢ ᐅ, ·ᐃᔭᐸᑕᐧᒃ ᓂᔭᔪᐤ ᐃᓴᑯᔪᐤ ᓇᑕ, ᐋᒋ ᒋᒥᑕᔨᒡ ᓇᑕ; ·ᐃᔭᐸᑎ:ᒪᑦx ᒻᒻᒻx

ᐊᑎ ᐅᐱᑕᑦ ᓂ, ᐊᑯᑕ ᓇᑕ ᑭ·ᐃ ᐋᐱᓇᐋ, :ᑲ ᑐᐋᑦx ᒥ ᓴ:ᑲᐊᐤ, ᒥ ᒋ ᐋᐱᓇᐤx

ᐊᑯ ᐃᑕᐤ ᒐᐧᑲᐸᐢ ᓂᔭᔪᐋ ᐃᐢ:ᑲᐋ, “ᒋᐸ ᒥᑕᑕᐋᐤ ᐊ ᒋᑲ·ᐃᐋᐤ ᓂᐸᐃᒃ?” ᐃᑕᐤx

“ᓂᐸᐊᒃ!” ᐃ:ᑕᐧᑲᑐᐋᐤ ᐅᐋx “ᒋᐸᒐ ᐊᓐ ᑐᑐᐋᐤ ᒋᒋᐋ ᑲ ᒪᔨᐃᒐᑦ,” ᐃᑕᐤx “ᒋᐸ ᒋ ᓂᑕ ᓂᐸᐊᐤ,” ᐃᑕᐤx

“ᓇᒪ,” ᐃᑕᐅᒡ ᐅᒡ ᐃᐢ:ᑲᐅᒡ, “ᒥ ᓂᐸᒐ ᒥᑕᑕᓇᓐ ᐊᑐᐋᑦ ᒪᓐ ᓇᐸᐋ; ᐊᑎ ·ᐃ ·ᐃᒋᒥᒋᒋ, ᓴᐢ :ᑲ ᓂᐸᐊᑦ,” ᐃᑕᐅᒡx

ᐋᒋᐱᑎ:ᒪᒡ ᐊᓂᔭ ᒥᐢᑎᑯᔪᐤ ᓂᔭᔪᐤ ᐋᑎᑕᒪᐋᒡ ᐅᑲ·ᐃᐋ, ᐅᑕ ᐅᑎᐢᒋᑕᓂᔨᒡ ᐋᑎᑕᒥᐢᑕᐋᒡx ᐋᑎᑕᒥᐢᒋᑕᐅᓇᐋᒡ; ᐅᑎᐢᒋᑕᓂᔨᒡ ᐅᑲ·ᐃᐋx

“ᒥ ᓂᐸ ᒐ ᒥᑕᑕᓇᓐ ᐊᑐᐋᑦ ᐊᐋᔪᐋ; ᐋ ᐧᐃᒋᒥᒋ:ᑕᐧᐃ ᓇᐸᐋ ᓇᐸᐊᑦ,” ᐃᑎᑯᐤ ᐅᑕᓂᓴ᙮

“ᓂᑕᓂᔅ! ᐊᑲ ᐱᑎᒪ ᑐᑐᐅᒄ! ᑲᐱᑦ ᑐᑐᐅᒄ!” ᐃᑕᐤ᙮

ᒥᔭᓴᐊᑦ ᐊᓐ ᒐᐧᑲᐸᔅ᙮

ᐋᐸᑎ:ᒪᐤ ᑕᓐᑕ ᒐᐧᑲᐸᔅ ᓂᔭᔪᐋ ᐅᑦᐧᐃᔅᑯᒥᔪᐤ ᓇᑕ ᐋ ᐋᐱᓂᑯᑦ, ᓇᔭ ᒐᒥᑕᔨᒋ ᓇᑕ᙮

ᐊᑯᑕ ᐊᓐᑕ ᐊᑎ ᐃᔅᐱᑕᑦ᙮ ᐋᑎᓇᑦ ᐅᔭᔪᐋ, ᐅᔭᔪᐋ ᒥᔭᓯᐃᑯᑦ ᐅᔭᔪᐋ ᐊᒐᓂᔅ:ᑲᐋ ᒐᐧᑲᐸᔅ᙮ ᐊᑯ ᐅᑕ ᐋᒋ ᐱᔅᑎᓇᑦ ᐅᓱᑭᓂᔨᒡ; ᐊᑯᑕ ᐅᑕ ᐋᒋ ᓴᐳᓯ[illegible]ᑦ ᐅᑕ ᐅᓱᑭᓂᔨᒡ, ᐋᒋ ᓴᐳᒋᓂᔨᒋ᙮

:ᑲ ᐃᑎᐱᑦ, ᒥ ᒋ ᐊᒋᐤ, ᒥ ᒋ ᐊᒋᔅᑎᒻ ᐅᑦᐧᐃᔅᑯᒻ᙮ ᒻᒻᒻ᙮

ᐊᑯ ᐃᑕᐤ ᒐᐧᑲᐸᔅ, “ᒋ ᒥᑕᑕᐋᐤ ᐊ ᒋᑲᐧᐃᐋᐤ?” ᐃᑕᐤ᙮

ᒻᒻᒻ᙮ “ᓇᒪ,” ᐃᑎᑯᐤ, “ᒥ ᓂ ᒥᑕᑕᓇᓐ,” ᐃᑎᑯᐤ᙮ ᐋᒋᐱᑎᒥᔨᒋ ᒥᔅᑎᑯᔪᐤ ᐋᑎᑕᒪᐊᒥᔨᒋ ᐅᔅᑎ:ᑲᓐ᙮

ᐊᐅ:ᑲᔭ, ᓇᐸᐃᑯᑦ ᐅᑕᓂᓴ᙮

• • •

ᐊᑯ ᐃᑕᐤ ᒐᐧᑲᐸᔅ, “ᓂᒥᔅ ᐊᓐᑕ ᑕᐤ,” ᐃᑕᐤ᙮ “ᒋᐸ ᓂᑐᐋᐱᒪᐋᐤ, ᒋᐸ ᐧᐃᒐᐅᓇᐤ; ᐊᑯ ᒋᐸ ᑕᐱᑐᐧᐃᓇᓄᐤ, ᒋᐸ ᑭᓄᐋᔨᒥᑯᐋᐤ,” ᐃᑕᐤ᙮

“ᓂᐦᐃ,” ᐃᑎᑯᐤ᙮ ᒐᑐᑕᒃ, ᓇᑐᐋᐱᒪᒃ᙮

ᒻᒻᒻ᙮ ᐱᔭᒋ ᑎᑯᓯᐧᒃ, “ᓂᒥᓴ, ᓂ ᐸᓱᐋᐅᒡ ᐅᒡ ᒋᐧᐃᒐᐋᑭᓂᒡ ᒐ ᓯ:ᑕᕆᒥ:ᑕᐤ,” ᐃᑕᐤ ᐅᒥᓴ᙮ ᐅᑕ ᐋᒋ ᓴᒋᐋᐱᕆᒋ ᐊᐅᒄ ᐅᔭ ᓇᐳᐄᕆᒋ ᐃᔅ:ᑲᐋ ᓂᓯᔪᐋ᙮

“ᓇᓯ,” ᐃᑎᑯᐤ, “ᐱᔅᐱᓇ ᒋ ᓂᐸᐃᒪᒐᓂ ᐅᑲᐄᐋ?”

“ᓂ ᓂᐸᐃᒪᐋ ᓂᔭ,” ᐃᑕᐤ, “ᓂ ᐄ ᒪᔭᕆᒥᑯᔪᐋ,” ᐃᑕᐤ᙮ ᐸᒐᑦ ᒐᐧᑲᐸᔅ, :ᑲ ᐃᓯᑲᐳᐅᒡ ᐊᓐᒡ ᐃᔅ:ᑲᐅᒡ᙮ “ᓂᒥᓴ,” ᐃᑕᐤ, “ᐱᑕᑎᓴᐅᒡ,” ᐃᑕᐤ᙮ ᐊᑯ ᐊᓐ ᐃᔅ:ᑲᐤ ᐊᔪᑕᐱᑕᐧᒃ᙮ “ᐱᒐᒄ,” ᐃᑕᐤ, “ᐸᑐᑕᒄ,” ᐃᑕᐤ᙮

ᐸᒐᕆᒋ, ᐸᑎᑲᐊᑦ᙮

ᐊᑯ ᒐᒃ ᐋᒋᒪᔅᑦ ᐊᑯ᙮ ᐊᑯ ᐊ ᐃᑕᑦ᙮

4. ᒐᐧᑲᐸᔅ ᑭᔭ ᒥᒋ ᐃᔦᒃ

ᐎᔭᐱᓂᔩᒃ ᒥᓐ, ᐱᔭᑐᐙᑦ ᐊᐙᔦᐙ ᐊᓐᑕ; ᐸ:ᑲᐃᒐᐎᔩᒋ ᒥᔅᑯᒥᒃ× ᒥᔅᑎᒥᔅ:ᑲ ᓇᒋᐧᑲᐙᔦᐙ× ᐱᔭᑐᐙᑦ ᒪ:ᑕᓯᑯᑕᐃᒐᔩᒋ×

ᒪᒪᒪ "ᓂᒥᔅ, ᐊᐙᓐᒋ ᒪᓇᑕ ᑭ ᒥ:ᑕᓯᑯᑕᐃᒐᑎᑭᒋ ᐊᓐᑕ?"

"ᐊᑲ ᑐᑐᐅᒃ ᓇᓯ, ᐊᑳᐃᔾ ᓂᑐᐙᐱᒥᒃ; ᒥᔅᑎᒥᔅ:ᑲ ᐊᓐᒃ ᓇᒋᐧᑯᐙᐅᒃ× ᐅᑎᓂᒥᔅ:ᑲᐊᐅᒃ ᐃᔦᐙ ᐙᑎᑎᑯ:ᑖ, ᐊᑯ ᐸᑭᔅᑐᐙᐱᑎᑯᔩᒋ ᒥᔅᑎᒥᔅ:ᑲ, ᐊᑯ ᐙᓯᓇᐙᒃ×"

"ᓂ"ᐃ," ᐃᑕᐤ×

"ᒥᒋ ᐃᔦᒃ ᐊᓐᒃ×" ᒪᒪᒪ×

ᐙᐙᑕᔅᐱᔑᑦ× ᒪᒪᒪ×

"ᓂᒥᔅ," ᐃᑕᐤ, "ᓂᑭ ᓇᓂᑐᐙᐱᒪᐅᒃ ᒪ ᐊᓂᔅᒋᑯᒐᓯᒃ," ᐃᑕᐤ× "ᓂᑭ ᓇᒋᐧᑯᐙᐅᒃ," ᐃᑕᐤ×

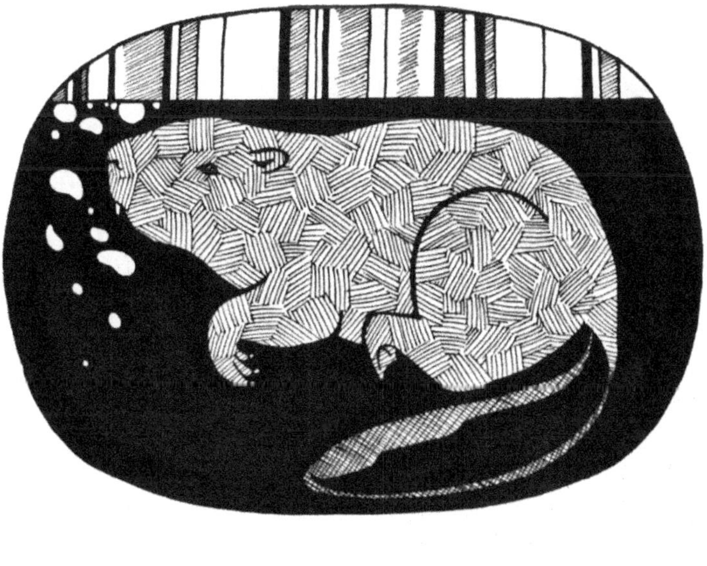

ᒼᒼᒼ᙮ ᐑᐱᒡ ᑲ ᐊᑎ ᐊᑯᐚᐢᑯᓯᐧᐠ, ᐊᑯᑕ ᐊᑎ ᐢᑐᑕᑦ ᐊᐣᑕ ᓇᑐᐚᐱᒪᑦ; ᐸᑐᐚᐤ ᐊᐣᑕ ᑕᐣᑕ ᒪ:ᑕᓯᑯᑕᐃᒐᔨᒋ᙮

• • •

ᐊᐅᑯᓂ ᐅᔭᔦᐚ ᑲ ᓄᒋᐧᑯᐚᔨᒋ ᒥᐢᑎᒥᐢ:ᑲ, ᐱ:ᑲᔨᒐᔦᐚ᙮

“ᒼᒼᒼ᙮ ᒪᐣᑕᐤ ᐚᑎᑕᐠ, ᒪᐣᑕᐤ᙮” ᓴᐢ ᒋ ᒋᐸᐚᐅᒡ ᐅᒡ ᐅᑕ ᐑᐢᑎᔨᒡ, ᐊᒥᐢ:ᑲ ᒥᐢᑎᒥᐢ:ᑲ᙮ “ᐅᑎᓂᒥᐢ:ᑲᐃᐧᐠ,” ᐃᑕᐅᒡ᙮

ᓴᐢ ᑭᐹ ᑲ ᐸᑐᐚᑦ ᐅᒥᓴ ᑲ ᐃᑕᒋᒪᔨᒋ᙮ ᒼᒼᒼ᙮

“ᐅᑎᓂᒥᐢ:ᑲ, ᓂ:ᑕᑭᒥᓂᒡ; ᓴᐢ ᐅᒋ ᒋ ᒋᐸᐚᑭᓄᐅᒡ,” ᐃᑕᐅᒡ᙮ ᒼᒼᒼ᙮

:ᑲ ᐊᑎ ᐱᑕᔭᑯᓂᒋᐱᔨᐅᓯᑦ ᒋᑭᓴᒼ᙮ ᓇ:ᑕᑭᒥᓇᑦ ᓂᔭᔦᐚ ᐊᒥᐢ:ᑲ, ᓇᑕ ᓇ:ᑕᑭᒥᓂᒐᑦ᙮

ᓇᐊᒻ ᐅᔭᔦᐤ ᐅᓱᔦᐤ ᐅᔭᔦᐋ ᐊᔅ:ᑲᔨᒡ ᐅᔭᔦᐤ ᐅᓱᔦᐤ, ᐊᑯᑕ ᐅᑕ ᐋᒋᔨᒋᓇᑦ ᐋᒋ ᐅᒋᐱᑕᑦ᙮ ᐊᑯ ᐅᔭᔦᐋ, ᐅᑦ ᐊᒐᐱᔭ; ᐅᑦ ᐊᒐᐸᔅ:ᑲ ᐅᔭᔦᐋ ᒥ ᐱᔅᑎᓇᐤ ᐅᑦ ᐊᒐᐸᔅ:ᑲ᙮ ᐊᐅᑯᓂ ᐋᒋ ᐱᔅᑎᓇᑦ ᐋᒋ ᐅᑕᒥᔅᑎ:ᑲᓇᐋᑦ ᐊᓐᑕ ᐊ ᐋᐱᓇᑦ᙮

ᒥᓐ ᓇ:ᑕᑭᒥᓂᒐᑦ, ᒥᓐ ᐋᒋ ᐅᑎᓇᑦ ᑯᑎᑲ᙮ ᐃᔭᐱᒡ :ᑲ ᑐᐋᑦ; ᐋᑎᑕᒥᔅᑎ:ᑲᓇᐋᑦ ᐊᓐᑕ ᐊ ᐋᐱᓇᑦ, ᓂᔨᔦᐋ᙮

ᐊᑯ ᐅᔭᔦᐋ ᐅᑦ ᐊᒐᐸᑐᔾ, ᐅᑦ ᐊᒐᐸᔅ:ᑲ ᒪᓇᑦ ᐅᑦ ᐊᒐᐸᑐᔾ, ᓇ:ᓴᐱ·ᑲᑕᑦ ᓂᔭᔦᐋ ᐅᑦ ᐊᒥᔅᑯᒪ, ᓴᑲᐱᑕᑦ ᐹᔅᑐᐅᑕᑦ᙮ ᐊᐊ, ᒐᑐᑕᑦ᙮

• • •

"ᐊᑯ ᑕᓐ ᐊᑎᑦ ᐊᓐ ᐊᑯ? ᑭ ᒋᑐᐅᑕᐋ ᒋᑦ ᐊᒥᔅᑯᒥᓗᐋ᙮ ᓇᑎ·ᒄ! ᒥᓂᒥ·ᒄ!" ᐃᑕᑭᓗᐅᒡ ᐊᓐᒡ ᐅᔅᒋᓂᔅᒋᓱᒡ᙮

ᓂᔭᑕᒡ, ᐃᔭᔨᑐᐤ ᐅᑕ ᐅᒋ ᐱᒍᑕᔦᐋ᙮ ᐋᐋᒡ ᑭ ᐊᐱᔨᓯᐋ, ᑭ ᒥᒪ·ᑭᓴᒪᓯᐋ :ᑲ ᐃᔨᓇᑯᔨᑦ᙮ ᒻᒻᒻ᙮

"ᐃᔭᐅᒄ, ᐃᔭᐅᒄ᙮ ᒐᑐᐅᑕᓂᒄ᙮"

"ᒐ:ᑲᓐ ᐋᒋ ᐅᑎᓂ:ᑕᐤ ᓂᑦ ᐊᒥᔅᑯᒥᓇᓐᒡ? ᐸᓯᐅᒡ!" ᐃᑎᑯᐤ᙮ ᒻᒻᒻ᙮

"ᒐ:ᑲᓐ ᐋᒋ ᐅᑎᓂ:ᑕᐤ?" ᐃᑎᑯᒄ, "ᐸᓯᐅᒡ!" ᐃᑎᑯᐤ᙮

"ᒐᑐᐅᑕᓂᒄ, ᒐᑐᐅᑕᓂᒄ᙮ ᐃᑐᐤ ᐅᑕ ᐅᒋ ᐅᑎᓂ·ᑯᒡ᙮"

ᐊᑯ ᐅᑕ ᐃᑐᐤ ᐋᒋ ᐅᑎᓇᔨᒋ᙮

ᐱᒪ·ᑯᓇᐱᑕᔨᑦ ᐅᔭᔦᐋ ᐸᐃᒄ, ᒥᓐ ᑯᑎᒋᔦᐤ᙮ ᐊᑯ ᒥ ᒋ ᐊᒋᐱᑕᔦᐋ ᑕᓐᑕ ᐅᑕ ᐱᐸᔨᒋᓂ:ᒪᐤ ᐅᑕ ᐅᑎᒋᔦᐋ,

ᐱᐱᒪᐧᑯᓇᐱᑕᐤ᙮ ᒥᐣ ᑯᑎᑲ᙮ ᐊᑯ ᒥ ᒋ ᐄᔭᐢ ᑐᑕᑯᐤ, ᑕᐣᑕ ᐅᑕ ᐱᐱᒪᐧᑯᓇᐱᑕᐤ ᐱᐸᓯ:ᑲᐱᓇᐱᑕᐤ᙮

ᒐᐋᔨᒋ᙮ ᒻᒻᒻ᙮

“ᐋᐸᑎᒼ ᐊᓯᓇ:ᑲᐃᒥᐟ! ᓂᐟ ᐊᑎ ᐄ ᒐᑐᐅᑕᓇᓇᐣ ᒋᐟ ᐊᒥᐢᑯᒥᓄᐋ ᓂᔭᐧᑲ ᒐᒍᑎᐟ᙮ ᐋᐸᑎᒼ ᐊ ᑐᑕᐧᒃ᙮”

ᒥᔨᑕᐤ ᐃᑎᒍᑕᐋᐤ ᐅᑎᒋᔪᐋ᙮

“ᓂᑐᐋᐱᒪᑕᐤ! ᓂᑐᐋᐱᒪᑕᐤ!” ᐃᑕᐅᒡ᙮ “ᒐ ᐄ ᑎᐸᐊᒪᓱᐋᐧᐠ᙮ ᓂᑐᐋᐱᒪᑕᐤ!”

• • •

ᐊᑯ ᐅᔭᔪᐋ ᐅᒥᐢ ᑕᑯᓱᐅᑕᐟ ᐅᔭᔪᐋ ᐊᒥᐢ:ᑲ, :ᑲ ᐊᑎ ᐸᐧᑯᓇᔨᒋ᙮ :ᑲ ᐃᑎᓱᒪᐟ ᑕᐣᑕ, :ᑲ ᐊᑎ ᐱᑭᐢᑐᐋᐋᐟ ᐅᐟ ᐊᐢᒋᐧᑯᒡ ᐅᑕ᙮ ᒻᒻᒻ᙮ ᐊᑯ ᐅᔭᔪᐋ ᐅᑎ ᐅᓯᒥᐢ:ᑲ ᐅᔭᔪᐋ᙮ “ᓂᒥᐢ, ᐊᑯ ᐊ:ᑲᓂᒡ,” ᐃᑕᐤ, “ᒐ :ᒪᒥᐢ:ᑲᔭᐧᐠ,” ᐃᑕᐤ᙮

ᐊᑯ ᓂᔭ ᑯᓇ ᓂᔭᑕᔨᒋ ᐅᒥᐢ, ᒐᒋᓇᔨᒋ ᑯᓇ, ᐱᔭᑐᐋᔨᒋ ᐊᐋᔪᐋ ᐱᔭ:ᑕᑎᒥᔨᒋ᙮

“ᓇᓯ,” ᐃᑎᑯᐤ, “ᐸ:ᑕᑎᒧᒡ ᐊᐋᐣᒋ,” ᐃᑎᑯᐤ᙮ “ᐱᐢᐱᓇ ᐅᒡ ᒋᑭ ᒐᒍᑎᓇᒐ ᐅᒡ ᐊᒥᐢᑯᒡ?” ᐃᑎᑯᐤ᙮

ᒻᒻᒻ᙮ “ᓂᒥᐢ, ᓄᑎᓂᒥᐢ:ᑲᐃᑯᒡ ᐅᔭᔪᐋ᙮ ᑲᑭᔭ ᓄᑎᒥᐢᑯᒥᐧᑲᑯᒡ ᓂᐟ ᐃᑕᔨᒪᐅᒡ᙮ ᓂᒥᐢ, ᐸᓱᐅᒡ ᓂᑕᓯᒥᒡ, ᓂᑕᓯᒥᒡ ᐸᓱᐅᒡ᙮

ᒋ ᑭᓄᐋᔨᑎᒼ ᒥᓯᐋ ᒐ:ᑲᓂᔪᐤ᙮ ᒪᔨᑯᐟ᙮ ᐊᐣᑕ ᐊ ᐋᐱᓇᐟ ᑎᐢᑐᐋᐃᑭᓂᒡ ᐋ:ᑲᐢᑲᔨᒡ ᐄᒡ ᐊᑯ ᐊᐣᑕ ᑕᒥᒡ ᐊ ᑕᐟ᙮

ᐋᑎᑕᒃ ᐅᒃ ᐃᔦᒃ ᓂᔭᔦᐋ ᒥᑊᐋᐱᔦᐤ᙮ ᒥ ᒋᐢᑯᐟᑎᒧᒃ ᒐ ᐅᒋ ᐱᒐᒃ, ᐄ:ᑲᓴᑲᔦᐤ ᑕᓐᑕ᙮ ᑲ ᐊᑎ ᐅᑎᑕᒪᐊᒧᒋ :ᑲ ᑐᑕᒃ᙮ ᒥ ᒋᐢᑯᔨᑎᒧᒃ ᑕᓐᑕ ᒐ ᐅᒋ ᐱᒐᒃ᙮ ᒻᒻᒻ᙮

ᐊᑯ ᐅᑕ ᐊᑕᓱᐅᐟ ᐅᑕ ᐱᑎᑭᒥᒃ᙮

“ᓂᒥᓴ, ᐊ:ᑲᓂᒃ ᐊᑯ ᒋᐟ ᐊᒥᐢᑯᒥᓇᒃ, ᑭᐢᒍᒐᓂᒋ᙮ ᐊᑯ ᒐ :ᒪᒥᐢ:ᑲᔭᐧᐠ᙮” ᐄ ᐱᐸᑕᐋᔨᒧᓱᐤ, ᐄᔭᔦᐋ ᐃᔦᐋ ᐅᑕ ᐊᑕᔨᒋ ᐄᐃᑎᒥᒃ᙮ ᒥ ᒋ ᐄᔭᐢᑐᑕᐧᑯᐤ, ᒥ ᒋ ᐱᑎ:ᑲᑯᐤ, ᑭᔭ ᒥ ᒋ ᐱ:ᑲᐊᒥᔦᐋ ᐄᒃ ᐊᓯᓇᑯᓂᔨᒃ, ᐄ:ᑲᓴᑲᔦᐤ ᑕᓐᑕ᙮ ᒻᒻᒻ᙮

ᐊᑯ ᐃᑕᐅᒃ, “ᐊᑲ ᐱᒪᔭᒪᑕᐤ,” ᐃᑕᐅᒃ, “ᓇᑭᑕᑕᐤ,” ᐃᑕᐅᒃ᙮ “ᐊᐢᑯ ᒐ ᐄᐧᑭᔭᓴᐧᐠ ᐊᑲ ᐃᑕᔨᑕᒐ ᐅᑕ᙮ ᐊᐢᑯ ᒐ ᐄᐧᑭᔭᓴᐧᐠ,” ᐃᑕᐅᒃ᙮ ᒻᒻᒻ᙮

ᓇᑭᑎᑯᐟ᙮ ᒻᒻᒻ᙮ ᐊᑯ ᒥᔭᒥᐢ:ᑲᐢᐟ, ᐊ:ᑲᓇᐟ ᐅᐟᐊᒥᐢᑯᒪ᙮ ᐊᑯ ᑲᒋᓯ ᒥᒋᓱ:ᑕᐤ, ᐊᑯ ᒥᓐ ᐋᑎᓇᐟ ᓂᔭᔦᐋ ᐅᑕᓯᒪ ᑲ ᐃᓯᓇᑯᓂᔨᒃ, ᒥᓐ ᐊᓯᓇᑯᓂᔨᒃ ᐄᒃ᙮

5. ᒐ·ᑲᐸᐢ ᒪᒥ·ᑯᑎᒋᑭᓱᐤ ᑲ ᑯᒋᐱᐃᑯᑦ

ᐊᑯ ᓇᐱᓂᔨᐠ, ᐊᑯ ᐅᑎ ᐃᑕ ᓇᐱᓂᔨᐠ᙮ ᐊᑯ ᐊᓱᐠ ᐋᒋᐠ ᓂᐱᐠ᙮

ᐊᑯ ᐃᑕᐤ ᐊᓇ ᐅᓯᒪ, "ᓇᓯ," ᐃᑕᐤ, "ᒐ ᐊᑲ ᓂᑕ ᐊᓐᑕ ᓂᐱᐠ ᐱᒧᒐᔨᓐ ᒋᑭᐢᒄ," ᐃᑕᐤ᙮ "ᑕᐤ ᐊᓐᑕ ᓂᒪᐢ ᒪᓯᑎᑦ ᐊᓐᑕ ᓂᐱᐠ," ᐃᑕᐤ᙮ "ᑳᐢᑕᑎᑯᓯᑦ," ᐃᑕᐤ, "ᒋᑭ ᓂᐸᐃᒄ," ᐃᑕᐤ᙮

ᒼᒼᒼ᙮ "ᓂᐦᐃ, ᓂᐦᐃ," ᐃᑕᐤ ᐅᒥᐢ᙮ ᑕᐸ ᒐᐢᑲ ᓂᐢᑯᒪᐤ ᐊᑎ ᐃᑕᒋ, ᑕᐸ ᑎᑕᐹᑐᐋᐤ ᐅᒥᐢ᙮

ᒼᒼᒼ᙮ "ᓂᒥᐢ," ᐃᑕᐤ᙮ ᒐᑐᑕᑦ, "ᓂᒥᐢ," ᐃᑕᐤ, "ᑯᐢᒐ ᒪ," ᐃᑕᐤ᙮ "ᒋᒋᐋ ᓂ ᐄ ᒧᐋᐤ ᓂᒪᐢ," ᐃᑕᐤ᙮ "ᑯᐢᒐ," ᐃᑕᐤ, "ᐋᐱᓂᑯᐢᒐ," ᐃᑕᐤ᙮ "ᐊᑯ ᐊᓐ ᒋᑦ ᐊᐱᑕᓯᑕᑭᓇᐢᒄ ᐊᓐ," ᐃᑕᐤ, "ᓂᔭᔦᐋ ᐅᑕᐱᑕᓯᑕᓂᔦᐤ, ᒥᐢᑎᒄ ᐊᓐᑕ ᐋᐢ ᒋᒥᑕᑭᓄᐤ, ᐊᑯᑕ ᐊᓐᑕ ᒐ ᐅᒋ ᓯᑲᐱᑎᒥᓐ ᐊᓐ ᒋᑯᐢᑭᓐ," ᐃᑕᐤ᙮

ᑕᐸᑲ ᓂᓇᐃᑕᑯᐤ ᐅᒥᓴ ᐊ ᐃᑎᓱᒪᒋ, ᐄᔭᐱᓂᑯᐢᒐᔨᒋ᙮ ᐊᑯ ᐅᔭᔦᐚ ᒥᐢᑎᑯᔦᐤ ᒐᒥᑕᔨᒋ ᐅᔭᔦᐚ ᐊᑯᑕ; ᐅᑕ ᒥᔭᑯᐱᑎᒥᔨᒋ ᐊᑯ ᓇᑕ ᐊᑕᐸᑭᐢᑕᔨᒋ ᐅᑯᐢᑭᐣ᙮

ᐊᑯ ᓇᑕ ᐸᐸᒧᑕᑦ᙮ ᒐᒃ ᐅᑎ ᐱᐸᒧᑕ, ᐸᒧᒐᑦ ᓇᑕ ᐅᑭᐢ:ᑲ ᓂᐱᒡ᙮ ᐊᑯᒥᓂᔨᒋ ᐅᑭᐢ:ᑲ᙮ “ᓂᑭ ᓇᑕᐚᐤ,” ᐃᑕᔨᒪᐤ ᐅᑭᐢ:ᑲ᙮ ᓂᔭᑕᐚᐢᑦ ᓂᔭᔦᐚ ᐅᑭᐢ:ᑲ᙮ ᒻᒻᒻ᙮

“ᒪᒥᐧᑯᑎᒋᑭᓱᐤ ᓂᑭ ᐚᐅᑭᒥᐠ!
ᒪᒥᐧᑯᑎᒋᑭᓱᐤ ᓂᑭ ᐚᐅᑭᒥᐠ!”

ᐃᓯᑕᓱᐤ᙮

ᐱᔭᑕᑯᑦ, ᓂᔭᑕᐅᑯᑦ᙮ “ᐊᐅᑯᐤ ᐅᐚ ᐸᒥᐢᑲᐢᑦ,” ᐊᐚᓂᐢ ᐅ ᐊᑯ ᐃᑎᑯᐤ, “ᐊᐱᓯᓱᐤ ᐊ ᐃᑎᒋ᙮” :ᑲ ᒋᐱᔨᐃᑯᑦ, ᒥᔭᑯᒥᑯᑦ᙮

“ᐊᐦᐊᐦᐊ!” ᐃᑕᐤ᙮ “ᐊᑲ ᒪᑯᒥ!” ᐃᑕᐤ᙮ “ᓄᑎᒥᑯᒋᐱᔨᐃ!” ᐃᑕᐤ᙮

ᒥ ᒪᑯᒥᑯᐤ, :ᑲ ᐊᑎ ᑯᒋᐱᔨᐃᑯᑦ᙮

“ᐊ"ᐊ!” ᐃᑕᐤ᙮ “ᐊᑲ ᐃᔅᐱᐃ ᓇᑕ ᐊ ᐧᐃ :ᑲᑎᔭᔨᓐ,” ᐃᑕᐤ, “ᓴᒋᔅ:ᑲᔨᒥ,” ᐃᑕᐤ᙮

ᐊᑯ ᐅᑕ ᐋᒋ ᓴᔅ:ᑲᔨᒥᑯᑦ ᐅᑕ, ᐅᑕ ᐅᑐᓂᒡ ᐋᒋ ᓴᒋᔅ:ᑲᔨᓂᔅᑦ ᓇᑕ ᐊᓐᑕ ᐅᑐᓂᒡ᙮

“ᐅᑕ ᓇᑕ ᒪ ᐊᑎ ᐃᔅᐱᔨ,” ᐃᑕᐤ, “ᓇᑕ,” ᐃᑕᐤ, ᐅᑕ ᐅᒥᓴ ᑲ ᐃᑕᔨᑎ:ᒪᑦ ᐅᑯᔅᑭᓂᔦᐤ᙮ ᐊᑯᑕ ᐊᑎ ᐃᔅᐱᔨᔨᒋ ᑕᐹ, ᓇᑐᐋᐸᑎ:ᒪᑦ ᐅᒥᓴ ᐅᑯᔅᑭᓂᔦᐤ ᐧᐃᔭᐸᑕᐧᒃ ᐊᔅᑕᔨᒡ ᐅᒥᓴ ᐅᑯᔅᑭᓂᔦᐤ᙮

ᐃᑕᐤ, “ᐊᓂᔭ ᒪ ᐊᓐᑕ ᒐ:ᑲᓐ ᑭᔅᑕᐋ,” ᐃᑕᐤ᙮ “ᒋᐋᐱᔨ ᒪ᙮” ᐃᑕᐤ᙮ ᐊᑯ ᒥᓐ ᒐᐋᐱᔨᒋ᙮

ᐧᐃᔭᐸᑎ:ᒪᑦ ᐅᑕ, ᒪᓐ ᑭᔅᑕᐋ ᒐ:ᑲᓐ᙮ “ᓇᑕᐊ,” ᐃᑕᐤ᙮ ᓂᔭᑕᐊᒥᔨᒋ᙮

“ᐅᑕᑕ,” ᐃᑕᐤ᙮ ᐋᑕᑎᒥᔨᒋ᙮

ᓴᔅ ᒥᒄ ᒧᔅᑎᓂ:ᒪᐤ, ᒧᔅᑎᓂ:ᒪᐤ ᑯᔅᑭᓂᔭᐤ, ᒪᒪᒋᑯᓂ:ᒪᑦ, ᒪᒪᒋᑯᓂᒧᐋᑦ ᑭᐹ ᐃᓭᒋᔅᑎᒥᔨᒋ ᓂᓭᔭᐋ ᐅᑯᔅᑭᓂᔭᐤ ᐅᒥᓴ᙮ ᐊᑯ ᐅᓭᔭᐤ ᑲ ᐅᒋᑲᐱᑎᒥᔨᒋ ᐅᓭᔭᐤ ᐱᑎᑭᒥᒡ ᐅᓭᔭᐤ ·ᐃᒋᔨᒡ᙮ ᐃᓭᓭᒋᐱᑎᒥᔨᒋ ᐅᓭᔭᐋ ᐅᒥᔅᑎᑯᒥᔭᐋ᙮ ᒐᔅᒐᔨᒪᑦ ᓄᒋ·ᑭᒥᔨᒋ ᐅᑯᔅᑭᓐ ᐅᐋ ᐃᔅ:ᑲᐤ ᓇᑐᐋᐱᒪᑦ᙮

ᓂᓭᓇᔅᑲᓇᑦ᙮ ᐊ:ᑲᔅᑕᐸᑦ ᒥᒥ·ᑯᑎᒋᑭᓯᐋ᙮ ᓇᐸᐊᑦ᙮ ᐋᑎᓇᑦ ᒐᐋᑕᐊᑦ᙮

“ᐊᑯᑕ ᓂᒥᔅ ᒐ ᐃᓭᔭ·ᐃᑦ ᒐᔅᑎᓇᔅ ᒐ ᐱᔅᑭᓯᑦ, ᒐ ᐱᔅᑭ:ᓴᑦ ᐅᓂᒪᓯᒪ᙮”

ᐸᔅᑭ:ᓴᔨᒋ ᐅᓭᔭᐋ ᓂᒪᓴ᙮ ᐊᑯ ᐸᑐᔅ ᐃᓭᒋᑦ, ᓇᔅᒡ ᓇᑕ ᓇᑕ ᓂᒪᓴ ᐊᓯᓇᑯᓯᑦ, ᓇᔅᒡ ᓇᑕ ᐊ ·ᐃ:ᑲᓯᑦ ᓂᓭᔭᐋ ᓂᒪᔅ ᐊᓯᓇᑯᓯᑦ ᐅᑎᓭ᙮ ᐊᑯᑕ ᐊᓐᑕ ᐊᔅᐱᔭᐅᔅᑦ, ᐊᑯᑕ ᓇᑕ ᐊᑕᐋᑦ᙮ ᐊᑯ ·ᐃᓭᔭᐤ ᒐ ᒥᓯᒥᔨᒋ ᐅᑕ ᒥᓭᑎᓯᒥᔨᒋ᙮

ᐊᑯ ᓇᑕ ᐊᔅᐱᑎᒥᔨᒋ ᐅᑕᔭᐤ ᐅᔅᒋᐋᔨᒡ ᐋᒋ ·ᐃ·ᐃᐱᔨᐅᔅᑦ!

“ᑕᐹ ᐋᓴ ᓂᒥᓴ ᓂ ·ᐃᒐᑭᑎᓭᒥᒄ,” ᐃᑕᐤ᙮ “ᓂ·ᐃᒐᑭᑎᓭᒥᒄ ᒋᒋᐋ,” ᐃᑕᐤ᙮

“ᐋᓴ ᐅᓴᒻ!” ᐃᑎᑯᐤ᙮ “ᐊᑲ ᒋ ᐃᐹ·ᑲᓇᐋ᙮” ᐃᑎᑯᐤ᙮ “ᒪ ᒋ ᐸᑐᐅᓐ ᒐ ᐊᑲ ᓂᑕ ᐱᒧᒐᔨᓐ ᓂᐱᒡ ᐊᓐᑕ ᐸᒧᒐᔨᓐ ᒋᑭᔅᒄ ᑲ ᐃᑕᓐ?” ᐃᑎᑯᐤ᙮

“ᐱᔅᐱᓇ ᒋ ᒧᓴᐋᓇᒐ?” ᐃᑎᑯᐤ᙮ “ᒋᐸ ᓂᐸᐃᒄ ᐊᑯ ᒋ ᑯᒋᐱᔨᑯᒐ᙮”

ᒥᒋ ᓂᐸᐃᑯᐤ ᐃᓭᐱᒡ᙮ ᒻᒻᒻ᙮

ᐊᑯ ᐊ ᐃᑕᑦ ᒥᓐ ᐊᓐᑕ᙮

6. ᐅᑎᓇᑭᓄᓯᐋ ᒐᐧᑲᐸᔅ ᐅᒥᓴ

ᐊᑯ ᒐᒃ ᐅᑎ ᐱᐸᒧᑕ ᒥᓐ, ᐊᑯᑕᑦ ᐅᑭᔅᐦᑲ ᒥᔅᑎᑯᒡ᙮ ᓂᔭᑕᑐᐋᒧᑐᐋᑦ᙮ ᐊᑯ ᐋᑎᑕᒋ ᐅᑭᔅᐦᑲ, ᐊᑯ ᐳᑕᑕᑦ ᓂᔭᔪᐋ ᒥᔅᑎᐦᑲ, ᐊᑯ ᒥᓐ ᐊᑎ ᒋᓇ̈ᔅᑯᓯᔨᒋ, ᐊᔅᑭᔭᔅᒄ᙮

ᒐᒃ ᒋᒋᐋ ᐦᑲ ᒋᓇ̈ᔅᑯᓯᔨᒋ, ᒐᒃ ᓇᑕ ᐦᑲ ᐅᑎᑕᑦ ᐱᓯᐦᒪ᙮

ᐊᓐᑕ ᐊᑕᔨᒋ ᐊᔅᒋᔾ ᒋᐸ ᐃᑕᔨᑕᑯᓂᔪᐤ᙮ ᐊᑯ ᐊᓐᑕ ᐧᐃᔭᐸᑕᐧᒃ ᐊᓯᓇᑯᓂᔨᒡ, ᐸᐸᒧᑕᑦ ᐊᓐᑕ, ᐊᓂᔅᒋᑯᒐᓴ ᐊᐅᑯᓂ ᐊᑕᔨᒋ᙮

ᐊᑯ ᐅᔭᔪᐋ ᐱᓯᐦᒪ ᐊ ᐱᒧᑕᔨᒋ ᐅᒪᔅᑭᓇᔪᐤ, ᐊᐅᑯᔪᐤ ᐧᐃᔭᐸᑎᐦᒪᑦ᙮ ᒋᒋᐋ ᒥᐦᔭᔪᐤ ᓂᔭᔪᐤ ᐊᔅᒋᔪᐤ ᒪᔅᑲᐧᒃ᙮ ᒐᐋᑦ᙮

ᐋᓯᑕᑦ ᐊᓐᑕ ᓂ ᐊᓐᑕ “ᓂᐸ ᓂᐸᓇᓐ,” ᐊᑕᔨᑕᐧᒃ᙮ ᓂᔅᐦᑕᐤ ᐃᓯᓇᑯᑕᐤ ᐋᒋᔅᑎᓂᒐᑦ ᐊᓐᑕ ᒋᐸ ᓂᐸᐅᒡ ᓂᔅᑦ ᓂᔭᔪᐋ ᐅᒥᓴ᙮

ᐊᑯ ᐅᓭᔦᐚ ᐊᑲ ᐃᑕᑦ ᐅᓭᔦᐚ, ᐅᓭᔦᐚ ᐊᑲ ᐃᑕᑦ, ᓂᓭᑕᐅᑯᔨᒋ ᒥᒋ ᐃᔦᐚ ᐅᒥᐢ, ᐚᑎᓇᔨᒋ, ᒪᓇᔨᒋ᙮

ᐊᐅᑯᔦᐚ ᑕᐸᐊᒪᓱᔨᒋ ᑲ ᑭᒐᒍᑎᒪᑦ ᐅᑦ ᐊᒥᐢᑯᒥᔦᐚ ᒐᑕᐅᓭᔨᒋ᙮ ᐊᑯ ᐧᐃᐚ ᒥ ᐱᒪᐃᒪᔦᐚ, ᐅᒥᐢ ᒥᐠ ᒪᓇᑭᓄᔨᒋ᙮

ᑕᑯᓯᐧᒃ᙮ ᒻᒻᒻ᙮

ᐊᑯ ᐃᑕᐤ, “ᓂᒥᐢ ᐊᓂᓭ, ᑕᓐ ᐊᑎᑦ?” ᐃᑕᐤ᙮

ᒻᒻᒻ᙮ “ᑕᐸ ᑕᐤ ᐅᓭ ᒋᒥᐢ,” ᐃᑎᑯᐤ᙮ “ᐚᐢ ᐊᓂᓭᐧᑲ ᓄᑎᑕᐅᑯᓇᓂᒡ ᐃᔦᒡ᙮ ᒥᓇᐅᓭᐅᒡ ᓂᓭᐧᑲ ᒋᒥᐢ,” ᐃᑎᑯᐤ᙮ “ᒪᓂᓭᔨᑕ ᐊᐢᑲᐱᒥᒋᒡ,” ᐃᑎᑯᐤ, “ᓇᐊᒻ ᐊᐢᒋᒪᒡ,” ᐃᑎᑯᐤ᙮

ᒪᒥᒋᓱᐧᑲᐃᑯᑦ ᐧᐃᐚ ᑲ ᒥᒋᓱᒡ᙮ ᐊᑯ ᐃᑕᐤ, “ᓂᑭ ᓂᑐᐚᐱᒪᐤ ᓂᒥᐢ,” ᐃᑕᐤ, “ᓂᑭ ᓂᑐᐚᐱᒪᐤ,” ᐃᑕᐤ᙮ :ᑲ ᐊᑎ ᐧᐃᐧᐃᑦ ᒥᐠ ᐅᑦ ᐊᒐᐱᐢ ᑕᐧᑯᓇᐤ, ᑕᐧᑯᓇᐤ ᐅᑦ ᐊᒐᐱᓭ᙮

ᓂᔭᓯᐸᑦ :ᒪᓴᔅᑯᐸᑕᔅᑦ᙮ ᐅᔅᑎᐸᒡ ᐱᒥᐸᑕᓱᐤ, ᑕᐸ ᐅᑦ ᐅᐤᑐᐤ ᒍᔭᒻ ᐊ ᐱᒥᔅᑯᐸᑕᔅᑦ, :ᑲ ᐃᑎᑦ᙮ ᓯᔅᑲᐅᐸᑕᓱᐤ ᐅᑕ ᐅᑦ ᐊᒐᐱᔭ᙮

ᐊᐅ:ᑲᔭ ᒪᔅᑯᑎᔨᒋ ᑭ ᓱᓇᔅ:ᑲᑕ:ᒪ ᐃᔦᐤ :ᑲ ᐃᑎᔅᑦ ᐅᑎ ᐱᒥᐸᑕᓯ ᐅᔅᑎᐸᒡ᙮ ᑭ ᓱᓂᓱᓇᔅ:ᑲᑕᓱᐋ ᐃᓯᓄᐋᐅᒡ ᐅᓇᐸᒥᓱᐋᐋ᙮ ᐊᐅ:ᑲᓇ ᐊᔅ:ᑲᐱᒪᒡ᙮

ᓇᑕ ᒪᒃ ᐋᑎᒋᐱᑕᑦ ᐅᑕ ᐅᒥᓴ ᐊᑕᔨᒋ᙮ :ᑲ ᐊᑎ ᐱᒐᑦ ᒥᒋᐋᐱᔦᐤ᙮ :ᑲ ᐊᑎ ᓇᑕᑦ ᐅᒥᓴ, ᑕᐸ ᐅᓇᔨᒪᐤ ᐊᓐᑕ ᐊᑕᔨᒋ ᐅᒥᓴ, ᐋᑎᓇᑦ ᐅᒥᓴ, :ᑲ ᐊᑎ ᐄᐄᑕᐊᑦ, ᐋᓂᓇᑦ᙮

ᑕᐸ ᒋᔅᒋᔦᐋ ᐅᒥᓴ, ᒥ ᒋᔅᒋᔦᐋ, :ᑲ ᐊᑎ ᐅᑎᓇᑦ ᓯᑐᑎ:ᑲᒪᓱᐤ ᑕᐸᑲ ᓴᐱᓱᐤ ᒋᒋᐋ, :ᑲ ᐊᑎ ᐄᐄᑕᐊᑦ᙮

ᓇᑕ ᒪᒃ ᑲ ᐊᑎ ᓇᑕ ᓇᓯᐸᑕᐊᑦ᙮ ᐊᑯᑕ ᐋᔭᓯᑐᑐᐋᑦ ᐅᒥᓴ᙮ ᒥᒄ ᑭ ᐳᐳᑕᑕᓱᐋ :ᑲ ᑐᑐᐋᑦ ᐅᒥᓴ, ᓴᔅ :ᑲ ᐃᐹᐧᑲᔨᒋ᙮ :ᑲ ᐊᑎ ᒋᒋᐸᑕᑦ, ᐊᑎ ᒋᒋᐸᑕᑦ᙮

“ᑕᓐ ᐊᑎᔭᒄ ᐅ ᐊᑲ ᐄᔭᓯᑐᑐᐋᒄ?” ᐃᑕᐅᒡ ᐅᒡ ᐃᔦᒡ ᑕᐸᑲ ᒥᒐᑐᒡ᙮ ᓄᒋᐧᑯᐋᒡ᙮

ᐱᐱᐱ:ᒪᐅᒡ ᓂᔭᔦᐋ ᐊᑭᑕᔅ:ᑲ, ᓂᔭᔦᐤ ᐱᐱᐱᒧᐋᐅᒡ ᐅᑎ ᐊᑎ ᐱᒥᐸᑕᓯ᙮ ᓂᓇᐅᑎᓂᓱᐤ ᓂᔭᔦᐋ ᐊᑭᑕᔅ:ᑲ ᐱᐱᐱᒧᐋᐤ᙮ ᒥᒄ ᒐ:ᑲᓂᔦᐤ ᐊᓯ ᐅᑎᒋᓇᐧᒃ ᐊᓐ :ᑲ ᐃᓯ ᓂᐸᐊᑦ ᓂᔭᔦᐋ᙮

“ᐊᑲ ᑐᑐᐄᐧᒄ, ᐊᑲ ᑐᑐᐄᐧᒄ,” ᐃᑕᐅᒡ ᐊᓐᒡ ᒋᔅᓴᐃᔦᒡ, “ᒋᑭ ᓂᐸᐃᑯᐋᐤ,” ᐃᑕᐅᒡ᙮ “ᒋᒋᐋ ᓴᔅ ᒋ ᒥᔅᑎ ᓂᐸᐃᑯᐋᐤ,” ᐃᑕᐅᒡ᙮ “ᐊᑲ ᓄᒋᐃᑯᐄᐧᒄ,” ᐃᑕᐅᒡ᙮

• • •

ᐊᐅ:ᑲᓇ :ᒪᓴᐢᑯᐸᑕᓯᔨᒋ ᓂᐱᐦ ᐅᐢᑎᐸᐦ ᐱᒥᐸᑕᓱᐤ᙮ ᐊᑯ ᐅᑎ ᐱᒥᐸᔨᑐᑕᐤ, ᐅᒥᓴ ᐅᑕ ᐅᐢᑕᐧᑯᓂᑯᐤ ᐅᐢᐱᐢᑯᓂᐦ, ᐊᓐᑕ ᐚᐢᑕᐧᑯᓂᑯᑦ, ᐚᐢᑕᐧᑯᓂᑯᑦ ᐊᓐᑕ ᐅᐢᐱᐢᑯᓂᐦ᙮

“ᑕᓐᑕ :ᑲ ᐃᑕᑦ, ᐊᑯᑕ ᐊᓐᑕ ᐏᐢ ᑕᐧᑯᓂ,” ᐃᑕᐤ᙮ “ᒥᐠ ᐊ ᐃᓯᓄᔨᓐ ᐊᑯᓐ ᒐ ᐃᑎᔨᓐ,” ᐃᑕᐤ᙮

:ᑲ ᐃᔦᔨᒋ ᐅᑦ ᐊᐚᓯᒥᔦᐚ ᐅᑎ ᐱᒥᐸᔨᑐᑕᐤ, ᓴᐢ ᐅᑦ ᐊᐚᓯᒥᐧᑯᐚᑭᓄᔦᐚ ᒐᐱ ᓂᑕᐅᒋᔨᒋ ᐅᑎᐧᑯᑎᒥᓴ᙮

“ᓂᒥᓴ, ᐊᑲ ᐃᔨᐱᒐᑕ ᒪ ᐊᑯᐢ ᒋᐸ ᒥᑯᐢᑲᒋᐧᑯᐚᐅᐦ ᓂᓯᔦᐚ ᓂᑕᐅᒋᔨᒋ᙮ ᒋᐸ ᒥᒐᑐᐅᐦ ᓱᒃ ᐅᓴᒻ ᒋᑊᔨᐱ ᓂᑕᐅᒍᐅᐦ᙮”

ᐚᑕᒥᐢᑎ:ᑲᓇᐚᐢᑦ ᐏᔭᐱᓇᐢᑦ᙮ ᐊᐅᑯᓐ ᒥᐠ ᐊᑐᑐᐚᑦ ᐚᑕᒥᐢᑎ:ᑲᓇᐚᑦ ᓂ ᐏᔭᐱᓇᑦ ᓇᑕ᙮ ᒥᓯᐚ ᐃᔦᔨᒋ ᐊᐅᐠ ᒥ ᒋᐢᑲᑯᔦᐚ ᐅᒥᓴ᙮

ᑕᑯᓯᑕᐊᑦ ᐅᒥᓴ ᐏᒍᐚᐦ᙮

7. ᒐᐧᑲᐸᐢ ᑲ ᑕᐱ:ᑲᑕᑦ ᐱᓯ:ᒪ

“ᓂᒥᓴ,” ᐃᑕᐤ, “ᐊᑯ ᒪ ᒐ ᐢᑐᑕᔭᐧᒄ, ᒐ ᒋᑎᓯᒪᐧᑯᒡ ᐊᐋᓐᒋ ᐅᓴᒻ ᒋ ᒥᑯᐢᑲᒋᐧᑲᑯᓄᒡ,” ᐃᑕᐤ, “ᐅᑕ ᐊᑕᔭᐧᒄ,” ᐃᑕᐤ᙮ “ᓂ ᒥᐢᑲᓐ ᐊᓐᑕ ᐊᐢᒋᔾ ᒐ ᐃᑐᑕᔭᐧᒄ,” ᐃᑕᐤ᙮

“ᓂᐦᐃ,” ᐃᑎᑯᐤ᙮ ᐍᔭᐱᓂᔨᒡ ᒐᑐᑕᒡ᙮

“ᐊᐦᐊᒃ ᓂᒥᓴ, ᐊᐅᑯᐤ ᒐ ᐅᒋ ᓴᑭᒍᐋᔭᐧᒄ ᐅ ᒥᐢᑎᒄ,” ᐃᑕᐤ᙮ ᐙᒋ ᓴᑭᒍᐙᔨᒋ ᐅᔭᔪᐙ ᐍᐙ ᑭᔭ ᐅᔭᔪᐙ ᐅᒥᓴ᙮

ᐊᑯ ᐅᑕ ᐍᔾ ᐅᑕᒡ, ᐅᑕ ᐅᑕᒡ, ᐅᑕ ᐊᑯᑕ ᐙᒋ ᐱᒍᑕᐢᑦ᙮ ᐊᑯ ᐊᓐ ᒐᐢ:ᑲᔭᐱᒍᔨ:ᑕᐍ, ᐊᑯ ᐱᔭᐢᒋᓂᔨᒋ ᐊᓐᑕ ᐊᓐᑕ ᐊᓐᑕ ᐃᔭᒥᐱᔨᒋ ᑭᐹ, ᒐᐢ:ᑲᔭᐱᒍᔨᒋ ᑭᐹ᙮ ᐙᒋ ᓄᑎᓇᐢᑦ, ᐊᑯ ᒥᓐ ᐸᐢᑎᓇᐢᑦ, ᐊᑯ ᒥᓐ ᐊᑎ ᐢᑐᑕᔨᒋ᙮ ᐅᑕᒡ ᐅᑕ ᐅᒋ ᐱᒍᑕᔪᐤ᙮

ᓂᐢ:ᑕᐤ, ᓂᐢ:ᑕᐤ ᓂᐸᐅᒡ, ᓂᐢ:ᑕᐤ ᑎᐱᐢᑲᔪᐤ ᐊᓐᑕ ᐊᑎ ᐱᒍᑕᒡ, ᐊᓐᑕ ᐊᐢᐱᓴᔨᒡ ᐙ ᐃᑐᑕᒡ᙮ ᐊᑯ ᐙᑎᑕᒡ, ᑕᑯᓯᒡ ᓂᔭᔪᐙ ᑲ ᒥᐢᑲᐧᒃ ᐊᐢᒋᔪᐤ᙮ ᒻᒻᒻ᙮ ᐊᑯᑕ ᐊᑕᒡ᙮

“ᓂᒥᔅ, ᐊᐅᒄ ᐊᑯ ᓂ ᒥᔅᑲᓐ ᐊᔅᒋᔅ ᑲ ᐃᑕᓐ,” ᐃᑕᐤ᙮

“ᓂᐦᐃ,” ᐃᑎᑯᐤ, “ᑕᑶ ᒥ:ᔭᐤ,” ᐃᑎᑯᐤ᙮ ᐊᑯᑕ ᐊᑕᒡ᙮

• • •

ᐊᑯ ᒐᒃ ᓄᒋᐧᑯᐚᑦ ᓂᔭᔪᐚ ᐱᓯ:ᒪ, ᒥ ᒋ ᐚᐱᒪᐤ ᐊᓐᑕ ᐊ ᐱᒍᑕᔨᒋ᙮ ᐊᑎ ᐊᓐᑕ ᓂ ᒋᐱᔅᑭᓇᒡ ᐃᑕᐤ, ᐊᑯ ᐊᓐ ᐱᔭᒋ ᐸᓱᓇᑯᓯᔨᒋ, ᐊᑯ ᓇᐸᑦ ᓂ᙮

ᐊᑯ ᐸᒍᑕᔨ:ᑲᓂ ᐚᒪᔅᑲᑯᑦ᙮ ᓴᔅ ᒋ ᐱᒍᑕᔨᓯᐱᓂ ᐊᑎ ᐸᑯᐱᔨᒋ᙮ ᒥ ᒋ ᐚᐱᒪᐤ᙮

“ᐊᐚᒐ ᐊᑯᐤ?” ᐃᑕᔨᒪᐤ᙮

“ᓂᑭ ᑕᐱ:ᑲᑕᐤ, ᓂᑭ ᐧᐃ ᐚᐱᒪᐤ,” ᐃᑕᔨᒪᐤ᙮ “ᐊᐦᐊᒃ, ᓂᒥᔅ᙮” ᓇᑐᐚᐱᒪᑦ᙮ “ᓂᒥᔅ,” ᐃᑕᐤ, “ᐸᑕ ᐊᓐᑕ ᓯᔅᑎᒄ,” ᐃᑕᐤ᙮ “ᓂᑭ ᐊᐱᒋᑕᓐ,” ᐃᑕᐤ᙮ ᒻᒻᒻ᙮ ᐊᑯ ᒪᔨᑯᑦ ᑭᑶ ᓯᔅᑎᑯᔪᐤ ᐊᓯᓂᐧᑲᑕᐧᒃ, ᐊᐅᑯᔪᐚ ᒪᔨᑯᑦ᙮

ᑕᐸᑲ ᒥᓯᑕᐤ, ᒋᓈᐸᒋᑕᐤ ᓂᔭᔪᐚ ᐚᓯᑕᑦ ᐊᓂᔭ ᓯᔅᑎᑯᔪᐤ᙮ ᐳᐳᑕᑕᐧᒃ ᒐᒋ ᓱᐧᑲᐸᑭᓂᔨᒡ ᑭᔭ ᒐ ᐊᑲ ᒋ ᐃᔭᔪᐧᐃᑕᔨᒋ ᐊᐚᔪᐚ :ᑲ ᐃᓯᓇᑯᑕᑦ᙮ ᒐᑐᑕᑦ ᐅᓂ:ᑲᓐ ᐊᑯ ᑎᔭᐱ:ᑲᑕᑦ ᐚ ᓂᑯᑕᑦ ᓇᑕ ᐊ ᐱᒍᑕᔨᒋ, ᓇᑯᑕᑦ᙮

ᐊᑯ ᒐᐚᑦ᙮ ᐊᑯ ᓇᐸᑦ᙮

ᐊᑯ ᐅᒡ ᐅᑎ ᐃᑎᐱᑕᐤ ᐊᓐᒡ ᐃᔅ:ᑲᐅᒡ ᑕᐱᔅᑲᔨᒡ ᒥ ᓄᑯᓐ ᓇᔅᑎᔅ᙮ :ᑲᔅᑯᐱᑕᑭᓄᐅᑦ ᐅ ᒐᐧᑲᐸᔅ, ᐅ ᒐᐧᑲᐸᔅ᙮

“ᓇᓯ,” ᐃᑎᑯᐤ, “ᐚᐸᑕ ᒪ ᐊᓯᓇ:ᑲᒡ,” ᐃᑎᑯᐤ᙮ “ᑲ ᐃᓯᓇ:ᑲᒡ ᓂᔭ ᐊᑲ ᐃᓯᓇᑯᓄᐚ,” ᐃᑎᑯᐤ᙮ ᐚᓂᐱᔨᑦ, ᐊᒋᑲᔪᐤ ᐚᓂᐱᔨᑦ᙮

“ᓂᒥᓴ,” ᐃᑕᐤ, “ᓂᓂᑳᓐ,” ᐃᑕᐤ᙮ ᒐᐢᑭᑕᐧᐠ ᐅᓂᑳᓐ᙮ “ᐸᓱᐤ,” ᐃᑕᐤ, “ᓂᓯᑯᓯᒼ,” ᐃᑕᐤ, “ᑭᔭ ᓂᐟ ᐊᐱᑯᓯᒼ,” ᐃᑕᐤ, “ᑭᔭ ᓂᐟ ᐊᓂᐢᑭᑯᒐᓯᒼ,” ᐃᑕᐤ᙮ ᒪᐦᑯᐟ᙮ ᒐᑭᐸᑕᐟ ᒐᑭᓇᐟ᙮

ᐊᐅᑯᓂ ᐅᔭᔦᐚ ᐱᓯᒫ ᑕᐱᑳᑕᐤ ᐱᓯᒫ᙮ ᑭ ᐚᐚᐦᒐᐱᔦᐚᓂ ᑳ ᑎᐦᑭ᙮ ᒥ ᒋ ᒥᒋᒪ ᒋᒋᓈᐤ ᐊᐢᐱᐢ ᐊᓂᔭ ᒋᓱᐦᒋ ᑭᐹ᙮

ᐅᑕ ᐚᒋ ᐚᐱᓇᐟ ᐅᓯᑯᓯᒪ᙮ “ᐱᐢᑲᑕ!” ᐃᑕᐤ ᐅᓂᑳᓐ᙮ ᑳ ᐊᑎ ᐱᐸᑎᑯᐧᑭᓱᐦᒋ ᒥ ᒋ ᐱᐢᑲᑎᒥᔦᐚ, ᓂᐸᐃᑭᓱᔦᐚ᙮

ᒥᓐ ᐅᐟ ᐊᓂᐢᑭᑯᒐᓯᒪ ᐃᔭᐱᐨ ᑳ ᑎᐦᑭ, ᐃᔭᐱᐨ ᓂᐸᐃᑭᓱᔦᐚ᙮

ᐊᐱᑯᓯᓴ ᐊᓐ ᐅᐟ ᐊᐱᑯᓯᒪ ᑭ ᐳᐳᑕᑕᓱᐚ ᑳ ᑐᐚᐟ᙮ ᑳ ᑐᑐᐚᐟ ᐄᔭᐱᓇᐟ᙮ ᓇᐊᒼ ᑕᐚᐱᑕᓯᓂᔦᐚ ᐅᓂᑳᓐ ᒥᔮᑲᑎᒥᐦᒋ ᑳ ᐱᐢᒋᐱᐦᐨ ᐅᔭᔦᐤ ᐅᐱᐢ᙮

ᑭ ᐊᑎ ᐙᐙᔨᒐᐱᔦᐙᓂ :ᑲ ᐃᑎᔨᒋ :ᑲ ᐊᑎ ᒋᒋᐱᔨᒋ ᓂᔭᔦᐙ ᐱᓯ:ᒪ :ᑲ ᐊᑎ ᓴᑕᔭᔨᒡ :ᑲ ᐊᑎ ᒋᓯᑲᔨᒡ᙮

“ᐊᑯᓐ ᒐ ᐃᓯᓇ:ᑲᒡ, ᒋᑭ ᑎᐱᐢᑲᐤ ᓇᓂᑯᑎᓂᔾ ᐊᑯ ᓇᓂᑯᑎᓂᔾ ᒋᑭ ᒋᓯᑲᐤ,” ᐃᑕᐤ᙮

ᑕᑯᓯᐧᒃ᙮ “ᓂᒥᓴ, ᐊᑯᓐ ᒐ ᐃᓯᓇ:ᑲᒡ, ᒐ ᓂᐸᔭᐧᒄ ᑕᐱᐢᑲᒋ; ᒋᑭ ᑎᐱᐢᑲᐤ, ᒋᑭ ᐊᒋᑲᐤ, ᐊᑯ ᒐ ᓂᐸᔭᐧᒄ; ᐊᑯ ᒐ ᒋᓯᑲᒡ ᐊᑯ ᒐ ᐅᓂᔭᐧᒄ,” ᐃᑕᐤ ᐅᒥᓴ᙮

ᐊᐅ:ᑲᑭᓐ ᐙᒋ ᑎᐱᐢᑲᒡ, ᐃᓇᓄᐤ, ᓇᓂᑯᑎᓂᔾ ᐱᓯ:ᒪ ᑲ ᐊᒋᑲᐙ, ᐃᑕᒋᒧᓇᓄᐤ᙮

ᐊᑯᑕ ᐊᐢ:ᑲᔭᒋᒪᑭᓄᐅᑦ, ᐃᔦᐤ ᐊᑎᔦᐧᑭᓐ, ᐊᐅᑯᐤ ᒐᐧᑲᐸᐢ, ᒐᐧᑲᐸᐢ᙮

Châhkâpâs

A Naskapi Legend

1.

Châhkâpâs kiyâ Kâchîtuwâskw

Chahkapas and Kachituskw

As noted in the section in the introduction entitled Stories about Chahkapas, John Peastitute pronounces the latter name as *Kâ-chî-tûskw*, using three syllables, except in the song, where he sings *Kâ-chî-tu-wâskw*. However, other Naskapi adults pronounce this word *Kâ-chî-tu-wâskw* (with a *w* in the last syllable). The editors decided to use the storyteller's pronunciation, spelling it *Kachituskw* in the English translation and notes, used as a proper name, but writing *Kâchîtuwâskw* in roman and ᑲᒋᑐᐛᔅᒄ in syllabics, reflecting contemporary pronunciation.

Within the story, John Peastitute also uses dialectally distinct words for "black bear" when referring to the character of Bear: *Chisâyâkw* (Western Naskapi, East Cree Northern) and *Miskw* (Eastern Naskapi, East Cree Southern, Innu).

1. Châhkâpâs kiyâ Kâchîtuwâskw

Âku an îyuw âhtât antâ, mikw utânisa wîchimâw, kiyâ wîwa, kiyâ wîy, nistûuch.

Âku itâw, niyâyuwa utânisa, "Niki-iyân mâ âku niki-wî-ûsîhtân an chit-uwtinuw," itâw.

"Uskuya antâ tâyuwa antâ piskutinâhch antâ; âukuw ânch châ-nâtichîhch," itâw.

"Niki-minîhkumun," itâw. "Niki-ûsîhtân uskuwt," itâw, "châ-ut-uwtiyâhkw," itâw.

"Nîhî," itikuw.

Âku niyâyuwa wîwa, "Wîchâwî," itâw.

Châtûhtâch, wâchâwât.

Âku an iskwâs wîchiwâw aniyâ kânuwâyihtâhk.

Âku mi-tâyuwa âti-utâkusîyich ûhtâwîya. Âti-nituwâpimât, mâwâch. Âku an iskwâw chî-tâyuwa ut-awâsîma. Âskw mi-ûhchi-îyuw, îyuw, mi-ûhchi-îyuw, âukun an Châhkâpâs châ-isinîhkâtâkinûut, an awâs an châ-îyut.

Âku niyâyuwa Kâchîtuwâskw isinîhkâtâkiniyuwa. Âukunî wâtîhtikuch, nâpâhikuch.

Âku mûkuch kîpwâ nâpâhikuch. Âku an Châhkâpâs âtâkinûut, nâhtâuchit an awâs.

Mi-mûkuw. Mikw niyâyuw minipitikuw niyâyuw, niyâyuw antâ âhtât â-nîhtâuchit, mânâtâ wiyâpinikut. Âku niyâyuwa ukâwîya mikw muwâyichî kiyâ niyâyuwa ûhtâwîya; mi-tâyuwa.

1. Chahkapas and Kachituskw

There was an Indian living here with just his wife and daughter. There were just the three of them.

Now then, he said to his daughter, "Here's what I'm going to do. I'm going to try and build us a canoe."

"There's birch bark on the mountain over there. We'll go over and get some," he said.

"I'll strip the birch bark," he said to her. "I'll build a birch bark canoe," he said, "and then we'll have our own canoe."

"Yes," replied his daughter.

Then he said to his wife, "Come on, let's go!"

And off they went, the man and his wife together.

Now then, their daughter lived with them and took care of their home.

When evening fell and her parents still had not returned home, she set off to look for them. But they were nowhere to be found! Her mother was expecting a baby. Her baby had yet to be born, he wasn't yet born, this child who would be known as Chahkapas. Chahkapas, the child that was to be born.

In those days, there lived a monster called Kachituskw. And it was none other than this monster, this Kachituskw, that had happened upon the couple and killed them.

Indeed, after the monster killed them, it ate them! But the child known as Chahkapas survived.

Kachituskw didn't eat him. It had just pulled him out from where he lay growing inside his mother and threw him aside. And it ate the mother and the father. They were no more!

Âku châk nâsch ati-ûtâkusîyich nasch.
"Niki-nituwâpimâuch mâ âku nûhtâwîy," itâyihtim an iskwâs.
Châtûhtât nâtuwâpimât.

Âukunî uyâyuwa antâ wâtîhtimwât nâpâhikuyikwânî utâ awâyuwa. Ukâwîya nâstîs antâ mi-iskupukuyuwa châkwân. "Sâs niyâhkâ nipâhikusipinich awâyuwa," itâyimâw.

Âku niyâyuw ki-nânituwâpuwâ kwâ-ihtit an iskwâs nâtâ â-sisuwîhkwâkunikâyich niyâyuwa kîpwâ châkwâniyuw niyâyuw. Wiyâpâhtâhk nâtâ wâschâchikunâyich châkwâniyuw. Niyâtâhk, wâtinâhk. Âukunî, nâstunuwât awâsa antâ âhtâyichî. Wâtinât, piyâhkâpitimwât niyâyuwa âhtâyichî.

Âukuw awâsis antâ âhtâsit. Mi-pîkupitikuw tântâ. "Wâs âukuw nisîm kâ-tât," itâyimâw an iskwâs.

Âku, "Tântâ nipâh-chî-ûhchi-iyipîhchân?"

Âku an awâsis wâtinât aniyuwa usîma, âku antâ âti-iyâsit antâ châkwâniyuw, chî-tâhkunim châkwâniyuw. Aschîhkusiyuw âkutâ kâ-tâhkunâhk, âukuyuw niyâyuw pâhtâhwât niyâyuwa awâsisa. Âku kâ-pîhtâhwât âku yâyâhchîsiyichî niyâyuwa awâsa. Châpîchiwâhwâsit niyâyuw chipîchiwâhikiniyuw.

Âku châwâtâhât.

Âku nâtâ kâ-tikusîhtâhât âku chîhchiwâ châswâyâhchîyichî, yâyâhchîsiyichî.

Âku kânuwayimât usîma.

"Tântâ nipâh-chî-ûhchi-iyipîhchân?" itâyihtim.

Âku niyâyuw châk niyâyuw ut-aschîhkw niyâyuw, âkutâ antâ âti-iyâsit, antâ ut-aschîhkûhch.

Meanwhile, the girl realized that it was starting to get very dark. "I'll go and look for my parents," she thought to herself, and she set off to look for them.

And so she reached the very spot where they must have been killed. Of her mother there was absolutely nothing left. "The ones for whom I search, they must already have been killed!" she thought.

She looked at where the snow was all stained with blood, and, indeed, there was something there. She saw something sticking up out of the snow and went over to get it. And who was it but Chahkapas! That was when she realized it was a child that was lying there. She lifted him out, tearing open his resting place.

There was a tiny child lying there. He had not been torn to pieces. "This child is my little brother!" thought the girl.

Then she wondered to herself, "How am I going to be able to keep this little baby alive?"

She took her little brother and placed him inside the small pail she was carrying. And as she lay him down inside the pail, that little guy was moving around. She placed a cover on her pail to close him in.

Then she set off with him to go back home.

By the time she arrived, he was really showing how strong he was, kicking and punching with mighty little baby kicks and punches.

The girl tended to her little brother.

Then she again wondered to herself, "How am I going to be able to keep this little baby alive?"

She started keeping the little guy in her pail, right inside her pail. But he was always kicking and punching it open!

Piyânîhchuwâskimiyichî niyâyuw ut-aschîhkw; mâsitiyichî, mâsitisiyichî châk. Wâwâch, wâwâch chîhchiwâ châk chiyipichuw an awâs.

Âku âti-misitisit, âti-nîhtâwâyichî. Mmm.

• • •

"Nimisa ," itâw. Sâs kîpwâ kwâ-chischâyimât.

"Nâsî," kîpwâ itâchâ mûsinâw.

"Nimisa," itâw, "tântâ mâ wâhchi-nîhtâuchiyâhkw âkâ chûhtâwînânuwâ kiyâ âkâ chikâwînânuwâ?" itâw.

"Âukuw Nâsî, wâs niyâhkâ anch chûhtâwînuw kiyâ chikâwînuw, chî-nipâhikuch awâyuwa," itâw. "Âku tâmîhch antâ schî-ihtân chikâwînuw uyâhch," itâw. "Âku âskw mi-chî-ûhchi-îyun, âku nâpâhikuch awâyuwa. Âku mi-chi-pimâyimikusipin niyâyuwa kâ-nipâhikuch, chi-wâpinikusipin antâ.

Nâtuwâpimitân, mâskâtân," itâw, "âku châwâhtâhitân," itâw. Wâhtimuwât aniyâ â-tûtuwât usîma.

"Nîhî," itikuw.

Pâtus châschâyihtâhk an awâs. Mmm.

• • •

"Nimisa, niki-mitisânîhkâsun mâ," itâw.

Mmm. Châ-itikwâ tâpâ chî-kistutikuw umisa. Mâtisânîhkâsut. Mmm. Pâhchât.

The little guy was already getting bigger and bigger! Without a doubt, without any doubt at all, this child was growing up fast!

And as he got bigger, he got better at talking.

• • •

"Big Sister," he said to her, for he already knew who she was.

"Little Brother," was probably how she usually addressed him.

"Big Sister," he said, "how have we survived, when we have no father and no mother?"

"Well, Little Brother, this is what happened," she said. "Someone killed our parents while you were still inside our mother's body. You hadn't even been born when they were killed. Whoever killed them must not have cared about you, must have just thrown you away.

"I went to look for you, and I found you," she said, "and I brought you back home." She told her brother what she had done for him.

"I see," he replied.

And from that moment on, the child knew what had happened.

• • •

"Big Sister," he said, "I'm going to make myself a sweat lodge."

Whatever he decided to do, his big sister went along with it; she wouldn't say anything to him. He made himself the sweat lodge and went inside.

Tâpwâ, pâpâhtâkusût antâ umitisânîhch; antâ mâmuchîhkisut. Âku châk, "Âhâkâ, Nimisa, pîkuna, pîkuna!"

Pâkupitimiyichî uyâyuwa umisa umitisân. Chî-akunâham kwâ-tûtâkinûuch mitisân âsinîhkâtâch.

Âukuw âpit, sâs misituw. Mi-isinâkusuw niyâyuw kâ-isinâkust kâ-ispitist. Nâham îyuwa âspitiyichî sâs kwâ-ispitit â-isinâkûhut.

Mi-kistutikuw iyâpich umisa; tân chipâh-itikuw?

Âku châk, wâyuwît chiyâchisâpâyâyich. Mmm.

"Nimisa," itâw, "niki-iyân mâ," itâw. "Niki-minikâhwâuch mâ nikiskuch kiyâ nit-âhchâpîy," itâw.

Mikw apisîsuw, mi-nâsch ispituw îyuwa âspitiyichî. Mikw sûhchâyihtâkusuw, mikw kichâhchîhtuw chîhchiwâ.

"Nîhî," itikuw.

Âku châtûhtât.

Âku niyâyuwa wâchinâkinâhtikwa â-mîywâskusiyichî mikw pipichikâhwâw, mmm, kîpwâ chânwâskwâhât.

Âku niyâyuwa, niyâyuwa mistikwa nûtimâskusiyichî iyâhtikwa. Âukunî wâ-ukiskukâsut, mikw kichîhkâwâw. Mikw ûstikwânikâm mistikwâ âyâpisâskusiyichî; niyâyuwa iyâspitâskusiyichî mistikwâ. Utâ wâhchi-kichîhkâwât âukunî châ-ukiskutuwât. Mmm. Châwât.

Nistwâskwâhâw ukiskwa.

Âku tâpâkâ astwâkuw nî mîchimiyuw âkâ âhtâchî. Âku mâmîchisut kâ-pîhchât.

All kinds of noises could be heard coming out of there! He was getting really hot. Then he called to his sister, "Dismantle my sweat lodge now. Tear it down!"

So his sister tore down the sweat lodge, pulling off its covering. She took it apart. He had put a covering over it, because that's how you make a sweat lodge.

And there he sat, there sat Chahkapas, already fully grown! He had completely changed in size! He had turned himself into a fully grown person.

And even now his sister didn't say a word to him. What *could* she say!

Now then, the following morning he went outside.

"Big Sister," he said. "Here's what I'm going to do," he said. "I'm going to chop down a tree to make myself a bow and some arrows."

He was only little. He wasn't really as tall as an ordinary person. But he seemed to be strong and capable of hard work.

"All right," she agreed.

And then off he went.

Now then, from a fine tamarack tree he cut a long thin stick from which he fashioned his bow.

For each of his arrows he used a whole black spruce tree. He had only to whittle off the branches, shaping the ends into a head, for these trees were just the right length for making arrows. He cut away the branches and made his arrows. And then he went home.

He made three arrows.

Now then, his sister would make sure there was something for him to eat if she was not around. And when he came in, he'd eat and eat and eat.

Âku kâ-mîchisuch itâw, “Nimisa,” itâw, “nituwâpimich mâ antâ,” itaw, “nit-âhchâpîy,” itâw. “Niki-mûhkutâw,” itâw. Tâpâkâ ûhtâwâwa umûhkutâkiniyuw tikuniyuw, kinuwayihtimwâuch iyâpich.

Âku nâtuwâpâtâhk. Âukunî uyâyuwa ut-âhchâpîya mikw pipichikâhwâsipin mistikwa. Mmm.

“Chipâh-chî-wî-tûtuwâw, Nâsî; âku tâpâ-nîhtâ-isinâkuhwâkinûw âhchâpîy,” itâw.

“Âku pâsû âkus, pâsû.”

Pâhtikâhâyichî. Pâhtâyâskunimâkut. Mâmûhkutât châsâhât ut-âhchâpîya. Mikw mâmâmîhkutâw; tâpâ-wî-mimiyûhkutâw.

Âku itâw, “Wîwitisin,” itâw.

Wâyuwitisinâyichî.

“Pâchi-pîhtikâhâyich nikiskuch,” itâw. Pâhtikâhâyichî.

Mâmûhkutât mîn, tâpâ-wî-mimiyûhkutâw. Nâstîs mi-wâwâtîhkutâw utâ ustikwânimâhch. Mikw utâ susuwâskûhkutâsuw antâ â-pimâskusiniyichî. Âkutâ antâ mikw mûhkutât, chîhchiwâ kâchî-sûsûwîhkutât kwâ-isinâkwâhât. Mmm.

• • •

Âhâk, âhâk; âhâk âku, “Nimisa, châ-iyâyân.”

Châchisâpâyâyich wâyuwît, wâyuwît.

Wâyuwît tântâ wâwâtâyihtâhk kîpwâ pitimâ; wâyuwît.

After they had eaten, Chahkapas said, "Big Sister, go to that place and fetch my bow. I'm going to carve it," he said. (Apparently, their father's crooked knife was still there in their home. It had been kept for him to use.)

She went off to get the bow that he just fashioned from the tree.

"You should surely be able to make a bow, Little Brother," his sister said. "Bows are not made like this!"

"Just bring it to me!" he said. "Bring it to me."

She brought it inside, she poked the stick in toward him. And he carved and carved and carved until he had finished his bow. He left it a little rough, not quite perfect. He didn't want to carve it nicely.

Then he said to her, "Throw it outside!"

And she threw the bow outside.

"Now bring my arrows in," he said. And she brought them in.

Once again, he carved and carved and carved them, roughly, without taking too much care, leaving them a little rough around the tips. He carved them smooth along their length. Along the shaft was where he carved them smooth.

• • •

Now then, "Big Sister," he said, "here's what I'm going to do . . ."

The next morning he went outside, outside he went.

He went outside, and thought about what he was going to do.

"Nûhtâwîy mâniya kâ-nipâhikuwâkwâ awâyuwa, atuch kâkiyâ nichî-nituwâpimâw, nichî-nituwâpimâw," itâyihtim.

Châ-wî-tipâhamuwât ûhtâwîya. Mmm.

Âhâk pâhchât.

"Pâtâh, Nimisa," itâw, "châ-utâhchâpâtuyân," itâw.

Mâyikut apisiyuw.

Âku uyâyuwa utî-nûchîhkuwâh ukiskwa uyâyuwa, "Nimisa," itâw, "chûhtâwînuw mâniyâhkâ," itâw, "tân âsinâkusiyichî aniya nâpâhikuch awâyuwa?" itâw.

"Nâsî," itikuw, "wâsâ chîhchiwâ kustâtâyihtâkusuw; misituw chîhchiwâ," itikuw.

"Kâchîtûwâskw isinîhkâtâkinûw. Misituw chîhchiwâ," itikuw.

"Nîhî," itâw.

Mi-chistutâw; mi-wîhtimuwâw châ-nituwâpimât.

"Nimisa," itâw, "nâtâ mâ niki-nânituwâpimâuch anischikuchâsich," itâw. "Utâ michimâ niki-pipâmûhtân," itâw.

"Nîhî," itikuw.

• • •

Wîpich kâ-ati-stûhtât, nâtuwâpimât Kâchîtuwâskwa.

Niyâyuw mâk antâ niyâtimwât ûhtâwîya. (Tâpâ unâyihtimwâw antâ kâ-nipâhikuyichî.)

Niyâtimwât.

"Whatever it was that killed my parents, surely I should go after it! I should go and look for it!" he thought.

He wanted to avenge his parents.

Then he went back inside.

"Big Sister," he said, "bring me some twine so that I can string my bow!"

She gave him the twine.

As he was working on his arrows, he said, "Big Sister, what does it look like, the one who killed our parents?"

"Little Brother," she replied, "that thing is a really terrible thing, a really ferocious thing, a really huge thing!

"Its name is Kachituskw. It's really huge!" she said.

"All right," he said.

He didn't say anything more, and he certainly didn't tell her that he was planning to go and find Kachituskw!

"Big Sister," he said, "I'm going out to search for squirrels. I'm going to be wandering around nearby."

"All right," she said.

• • •

But as soon as he set off, he went in search of Kachituskw!

He drew closer and closer to the spot where his parents had been. (He knew exactly where that spot was—he was in no doubt about that.)

He went directly to the spot.

Âku antâ asinîyuw astâyuw mîhchâpiskâyuw. Âukuyuw niyâtâhk. Âku niyâyuwa ukiskwa kiyâyât nâtâ, wâhyuwîs nâtâ kiyâ ut-âhchâpiya. Âyikunikâhwât nâtâ. Âku niyâyuw asinîyuw niyâtâhk. Âku nâtâ tâhkûch nâtâ âkutâ pâmisîhk. Pâmisinist.

Nâkimust:

"Kâchîtuwâskw nitûnichâhâw,
Kâchîtuwâskw nitûnichâhâw."

• • •

"Mâh! Awân âku? Nitûhtuwîhkw mâ â-itwâut. Nituwâpim! Chisâyâkw, nituwâpim! Miskw, Miskw nituwâpim!"

Nâtuwâpimât Miskw. Mmm.

Âukunî uyâyuwa pâmisiniyichî asinîhch. Mmm. Châtutikut,

"Awâ u chiy Kâchîtuwâskw âtikuyin?"

"Nama." itâw, "namayâw nîy."

"Âhâk, chîwâmâ antâ," itâw. "Kâchîtuwâskw âukw," itâw. "Âukw nâtûnichâhak."

Tâkusîhk Miskw.

"Tân âhtit?" itâuch.

"'Miyâw chîy nâtuwâyimitân' kwâ-isit," itâw. "'Kâchîtuwâskw âukun nâtuwâyimik' kwâ-isit," itâw.

"Chîy mâ, chîy mâ, Wâpiskw! Nituwâpim!"

Nâtuwâpimikut Wâpiskwa.

Now then, there was a large rock sitting there, and that was what he headed towards. He hid his arrows there, next to the rock, and not too far from there he hid his bow as well. He dug-dug-dug down into the snow and buried them there. Then he went over to the rock and lay down on top of it. The little guy lay down.

And then he sang,

"Kachituskw he tries to meet,
Kachituskw he tries to meet."

• • •

"Listen! Who's that?" said Kachituskw. "Listen to that singing! Go look for him! Bear, go look for him! Bear, Bear, go look for him!"

And Bear went off to find out who was there.

And there was the little one, lying on the rock. Chahkapas called out to Bear.

"Are you the one people call Kachituskw?"

"No!" replied Bear. "I'm not Kachituskw!"

"Well, then, go on back home. Kachituskw is the one I want. That's the one I want to meet."

Bear arrived back.

"What happened?" the animals asked him.

"He said, 'You're not the one I want,'" Bear replied. "'Kachituskw is the one I want,' is what he said to me," Bear went on.

Then Kachituskw said to Polar Bear, "Hey you! You! You go see him!"

Polar Bear set off to go see Chahkapas.

Âukunî piyâtûhtâyichî, wîpich piyâchi-pâsunâkusiyichî, sâs kwâ-chitutât.

Itâw, "Awâ chîy Kâchîtuwâskw?" itâw.

"Nama," itikuw.

"Kâchîtuwâskw âukw nâtûnichâhak," itikuw.

Châwâyichî.

Tâkusiniyichî, "Tân âhtit?" itâuch.

"'Kâchîtuwâskw âukw nâtûnichâhak,' kuyât," itâw. "'Chîwâmâ,' âkwâsit," itâw. "Ni-chîwâtisâhuk."

Âku an Kâchîtuwâskw, "Tân âsinâkusit an?" itâw.

"Chîhchiwâ apisîsuw," itâw Wâpiskw. "Asinîhch antâ chîschinisuw," itâw. "Apisîsuw chîhchiwâ," itaw. "Ki-pisâpâchîwâsuwâ kwâ-isinâkusit," itâw. "Ki-chinwâpâchisuwâ kwâ-isinâkusit," itâw.

• • •

Âku, "Niki-nituwâpimâw," itâw Kâchîtuwâskw.

Pâsikut. Misituw tântâ, ki-nânâmipiyuwa aschîyuw pâsikut.

Mmm. "Âukw, âukw awîchâ." Tâpâ unâyimâsuw.

Niyâyuwa mistikwa siyâkwâskusiyichî âpîhtuwâskw nâtâ kwâ-îstikutâyich ustikwâniyuw, siyâkwâskwâhamiyichî.

"Âukuwîchâ," itâyimâw. Châtûstuwât, châtûstuwât, ki-nipisuwâ kwâ-ihtit, mi-âhchîsuw nâstîs. Niyâtât Kâchîtuwâskw, âukunî pâmisinisiyichî asinîhch tâhkûhch.

And as he approached, as soon as he was close to him, Chahkapas spoke to him.

"Are you Kachituskw?" he said.

"No," replied Polar Bear.

"It's Kachituskw that I'm trying to meet," Chahkapas told him.

And Polar Bear went back home.

As soon as he arrived, the animals asked him, "What happened?"

"He said to me, 'It's Kachituskw that I'm trying to meet,'" Polar Bear replied. "He said, 'Go on back home.' I was sent back home," he told the animals.

"What does he look like?" Kachituskw asked Polar Bear.

"He's really small," Polar Bear said. "He was lying on a rock. He's really small, and he looks skinny too. He seems to be all stringy-longy-skinny!"

• • •

"Well then," said Kachituskw, "I'll go and see him."

Kachituskw got up, and, because of its huge size, it seemed like the ground was trembling.

"That has to be Kachituskw," thought Chahkapas. He had no doubt about that.

Kachituskw was so tall that as it emerged from the woods its head was level with the midpoint of the height of a tree.

"That has to be Kachituskw," Chahkapas thought. The little guy lay perfectly still, so still he seemed to be dead, he didn't move at all. Kachituskw went up to him, to that little guy lying on top of the rock.

"Nâââ," itâw, "awâ Kâchîtuwâskwa kâ-nânitunichâhât?" itâw. "Nâstîs uwâ âkâ âyâpichinâkusuwâ âkâ chî-isinâkusuwâ," itâw.

Wâhchi-nitûhtâkust.

"Wâwâch uya sâs ki-nâstwâyihtimûsipinuwâ," itâw.

"Utâ wâhchi-utâhwât uya uschûn uya," itâyimikuw nâ iyâpich. "Kimâ wâhpischûnâmiyin nâtâ nikiskuch âpich," itâyimikuw. Wâhyuwîs nâtâ apiyuwa ukiskwa.

Wiyâpischunâmât uyâyuwa uschûn wâhchi-wâpiskuwât. Nâtâ nâhâw ukiskuyuwa âpiyichî, âkutâ nâtâ piyâschiniyichî; kwâ-chinistipikâpûsiyichî.

"Tântâ u niyâstwâyihtimiyichî," itikuw.

Ki-chîtâpimâwâ Kâchîtuwâskw. Mûschîhkûnichinâyichî ukiskuyuwa kiyâ ut-âhchâpîyuwa. Kâ-mûschîhkûnichinâyichî, châtutikut, "Nûhtâwîy mâ kâ-nipâhikuwâkwâ tân âspis miskûsiyichî," itâw.

• • •

Â-twâmuwât wâchinâkinâhtikwa chimisuyuwa, misîtichisuywa.

Wâtâchîstuwâyichî pâmwâyichî. Nâhâw misihwâw niyâyuwa wâchinâkinâhtikwa kwâ-pîsîtikâhwât.

"Tâpâ-ispis-miskûsiyuwa, mi-ispis-miskûsiyuwa," itâw Kâchîtuwâskw.

Âku utâ pâchinuwâkâpiskâyuw asinîyuw, asinîyuw piskutinâw utâ isinâkuniyuwa, utâ asinîyuw âstâyich.

"Mâw kwâ-ispis-miskûsiyichî," itâw, "niyâyuwa â-chîschâkâyich."

"Ahaaa!" said Kachituskw. "Is this the one who's been trying to meet Kachituskw? He really doesn't look like much to me."

That little guy, Chahkapas, just listened to Kachituskw.

"Unfortunately," Kachituskw went on, "he already seems to be completely overcome by fear!"

Chahkapas thought to himself, "It uses its trunk to suck people up. If only you'd use your trunk to lift me over to where my arrows are!" His arrows were lying quite far from him.

Then Kachituskw lifted him up with its trunk and flipped him down right next to his arrows. He landed right there where his arrows were. Chahkapas quickly picked himself up.

"Hmm," Kachituskw wondered. "How can he recover so fast if he was paralyzed with fear?"

It looked at Chahkapas, who was pulling his bow and arrows out of the snow. He pulled them out of the snow and said, "How strong whatever it was that killed my parents must have been!"

• • •

He pointed to a sturdy tamarack tree that was standing straight and tall.

He drew back the string of his bow and fired an arrow at it, hitting it dead on, smashing the tree to pieces!

Said Kachituskw, "That tree isn't very strong. It's not at all strong."

Now then, there was a rock facing them, a rock so big that it looked like a mountain.

Said Kachituskw, "Here's how strong that one you seek is. He's as strong as this rock face!"

Wâtinâyichî ukiskuyuwa. Pâmutimiyichî kwâ-nikisâkâhamiyichî.

Kwâstât, âukuyuw kwâstât.

Âti-chîwâyuwâpiyûut, tântâ pâikw iskunâyuwa ukiskuyuwa. Pâmukut âti-chîwâyuwâpiyûut nâutâ misûkuw. Kwâ-pîkusûkunâhukut aniya âtâhukut. Pâpâmitâchimipâhtât Kâchîtuwâskw.

Niyâtâyichî ukiskuyuwa, uyâyuwa kâ-pimuchâyichî, wâtinâyichî niyâtikut mîn kwâstâchâ wâhchi-pimukut.

"Nîhî tâpwâ," itâw, "tâpwâ chî-nipâhin," itâw Kâchîtuwâskw. Iyimihikuw tântâ. "Chî-nipâhin tâpwâ. Mmm. Âku mâw châ-tûtuwiyin: châ-pîkusuwiyin. Âku uyâyuwa nîhtûkiya uyâyuwa âukunî châ-minisimin," itâw. "Âukunî uyâyuwa châ-âpichîhtâyin," itâw.

Mmm. "Nîhî," itikuw.

• • •

Pâpîkuswât. Âku uyâyuwa wîhtûkâyuwa uyâyuwa âukunî uyâyuwa miyâwâyihtimwât. Mânisimwât, nâswâpîhkâtâhk; wîhtûkâma nâswâpîhkâtâhk.

Âku châwâtûutât.

Âku utâ piyâchi-pistûutât chipiskwâhch pâhchât.

Âku mâmîchisut, kîpwâ umisa mâyikut mîchimiyuw. Âku uya utî-mîchisûh, "Nimisa," itâw, "antâ mâ ni-pâtân châkwânîchânî, pîhtikitâh," itâw.

"Châ-nûchîhkimin," itâw.

Pâsikusipâhtâyichî umisa nâtuwâpâhtimiyichî âukunî astâyichî. Upiywâwîyuwâ châkwâniyuwa misâyuwa; â-sâpîwiyichî kwâstimiyichî.

Chahkapas took one of his arrows and fired it at the rock face, breaking a piece of it clean off.

Now Kachituskw was scared! Right then and there it began to feel afraid of Chahkapas!

There was one arrow left. As Kachituskw turned around, the arrow hit its hip, breaking it. It began to crawl, moving around this way and that.

Chahkapas went over to Kachituskw, pulled out the arrow he had just fired at it, and shot it again on the other side.

"Truly," said Kachituskw, "truly you have killed me!" He was talking to Chahkapas. "You have really killed me, and here is what you're going to do with me. Cut me up! These ears of mine, cut them off!" it said. "You'll be able to find a use for them."

"All right," said Chahkapas.

• • •

And so Chahkapas cut Kachituskw up into pieces and took the ears, which were left over and of no other use, for himself. He cut them off and tied the pair of them together.

Then he carried them home on his back.

When he got home, he took them off his back at the doorway and went inside.

Now then, he ate and ate and ate, because his sister gave him some food. While he was eating, he said, "Big Sister, I've brought something home, if you'd go and bring it in.

"Do something with it then!" he said.

His sister got up right away and went to fetch the stuff he'd left lying outside. They were big hairy things, and she stepped back, afraid of them.

"Nâsî," itikuw, "châkwâyuwa uyâyuwa?" itikuw.

"Chûhtâwînuw kâ-nipâhikuwâkwâ awâyuwa: niyâyuwa wîhtûkiyuwa âukunî niyâyuwa," itâw. "Ni-nipâhimâwâ," itâw. "Pîhtikitâh," itâw, "châ-nûchîhkimin," itâw. "Châ-unipâkinîhkûyin, kiyâ nîst pâikw châ-unipâkiniyin." Tântâ misâyukâyuwa.

Pâhtikitâyichî â-itisumât â-ihtiyichî. Âku nûchîhkimiyichî, âyukunî wânipâkinîhkâkut.

“Little Brother!” she said. “What are these?”

“The one who killed our parents, those are its ears,” he replied. “I killed it,” he said. “Bring them in and get to work on them. Make a blanket for me out of them, and make one for yourself as well.” (They were huge ears!)

She did as she was told and brought them inside. She set to work on them and made him a blanket from them.

2.

Châhkâpâs kiyâ Kâwâwâpisuwâhâch Awâyuwa

Chahkapas and the Swing People

2. Châhkâpâs kiyâ Kâwâwâpisuwâhâch Awâyuwa

Chiyâchisâpâyâyich wânît.

Piyâhtuwât; piyâhtuwât antâ awâyuwa antâ âhtâwiyichî. Mmm. "Nimisa, awâchânichî mântâ ki-mitwâwâpisutikichî?"

"Nâsî, âkâ nituwâpimich; wâsâ anch chîhchiwâ mi-ipwâhkâuch. Utîhtitwâwâ, âku châ-wâwâpisunisch.

"Âku kutuwâuch, antâ âkutâ nâtâ âstâch ut-aschîhkuwâw, misâyuw. Âku wiyâwâpisunâtwâwî îyuwa, niyâyuwa âspiyichî niyâyuwa, âku pâskâpâsimwâch niyâyuwa, niyâyuwa apisiyuwa. Âku niyâyuwa ut-aschîhkuwâw, niyâyuwa âkutâ nâtâ putâkimipiyichî. Âku âskwâsuyichî utâyuw niyâyuwa ut-aschîhkuwâw nâpâhikisuyichî."

"Nîhî Nimisa, mi-niki-chi-nituwâpimâuch. Chî-kustâchimin usâm â-itâchimuyin," itâw.

• • •

Wîpich kâ-wâtâspisut, nâtuwâpimât.

Âukuw wâhchi-sâkâskwâst, misitiyuwa ut-asâma kiyâ ut-âhchâpîya misitiyuwa, ki-apisîsisuwa kwâ-isinâkusit.

"Mâ! Mântâw wâtîhtâhkw. Wâwâpisunihîkw!" kâ-itikut umisa. Mmm.

"Wâwâpisû mântâw!"

Wâpâhtimwâw ut-aschîkuyuw âstâyich.

Âhâk, châmiyât nâtâ ukiskwa, nistiyuwa ukiskwa; châmiyâst nâtâ. Âku uyâyuwa ut-âhchâpîya, uyâyuwa uyâyuw ut-âhchâhpâskwa, âukunî mi-pistinâw. Âku

2. Chahkapas and the Swing People

One morning, Chahkapas got up.

He heard the sound of people nearby. "Big Sister," he said, "who do you think that is? Who is making that swinging noise?"

"Little Brother," she said, "don't go after them, because they are not very smart, those people. If you reach them, they'll make you swing.

"What they do is, they make a fire, and they sit their big pot on it. They put someone on the swing and while he is swinging they cut the rope! Then right into their pot the person falls! His body gets burned in the pot and he is scalded to death!"

"It's okay, Big Sister," he assured her. "I won't go near them. You've managed to scare me enough with what you've told me."

• • •

But Chahkapas, as soon as he had dressed himself, went over to visit the Swing People.

As the little guy emerged from the woods, he looked very small, though he had big snowshoes and carried a big bow.

"Listen!" said one of the Swing People. "We have a visitor! Make him swing!" This was just what his sister had warned him about.

"Swing, stranger!" they said.

He could see their pot sitting there.

niyâyuw châ-pâchi-chitûhtât niyâyuw, chî-usîhtâyuwa tûmîhkwâna umisa, chî-kinuwâyihtimiyuwa. Âukunî kâ-châmûtimât piyâpîhtâhâhk utâ utâ utîhkûhch; niyâyuw tûmîhkwâna, â-nîsinîyichî.

Âku utâ âtitâhk utâ utîhkûhch châ-pikwâtâut utâ, châ-âkâ-chî-pâchîhtât. Mmm.

Wâwâtipit chikisâm. (Mi-minâw ut-asâma, kiyâ ut-âhchâpâskwa tâhkunâw.)

• • •

Âku itâw, "Wâs mân châ-ihtûtuyâkw," itâw, "mâhân âkw chit-aschîhkuwâw," itâw, "châstinâs âkutâ nâtâ châ-pâchisiniyân châ-piskâpâsuyâkw," itâw. "Âku nâtâ pâchisiniyânâ," itâw, "pimîsuyânâ mâk," itâw. "Âku châ-wâskâpistûyâkw, châ," itâw. "Châ-nûhtâpuwâsiyâkw," itâw, "â-pimîsuyân," itâw, "niki-pimîsun chîhchiwâ." itâw.

Wiyâwâpîhchânikut, kîpwâ châsipiyit â-ispiyit uyâyuw.

Âku niyâyuw pâikw, niyâyuw apisiyuw, wâhtâpâkimuyich niyâyuw, wâhtâpâkimuyich upis. Pâsimiyichî uyâyuw apisiyuw nâham uyâyuwa aniyâ ut-aschîhkuyuw, âkutâ nâham piyâchisinist. Mmm.

Âkutâ nâtâ châ-muskâmuskâchûsust. Tâpâ nipuw, mikw ûhchi-îtâpimâsuw nâtâ, wâhchi-nânâkichâhât.

Kâ-itisumitâhkw, "Wâskâpistukw!" Wiyâskâpistâkuch. Âku misiwâ ki-nâtikûchî âtâyimât kâ-wâskâpistâkuch, kîpwâ kâ-kinuwâpimât.

Now then, he arranged three of his arrows so that they were standing up. Little Chahkapas set his arrows upright, but he did not let go of his bow. Before he had left home he'd stolen two little containers full of caribou fat that his sister had stored away. Now he took these out and put one under each armpit.

He strapped it under his arms like it was a belt, so it wouldn't slip out.

He sat down, still wearing his snowshoes, and tried to get comfortable. (He hadn't taken them off, and he was still holding on to his bow.)

• • •

He said to the people, "You're going to do something to me. There, in your pot," he said, "for sure when you cut the rope, I'll drop right into it. When I drop in there," he said, "I'll be all greasy. Then you'll sit down in a circle around me, and you'll stir the broth when I am greasy. I'll be really greasy!"

Now then, they were swinging him, he was going really, really fast, that's how he was swinging.

One of the Swing People was already there, next to the rope, at the end where it was attached. She cut the rope when he was right over her pot, and little Chahkapas dropped right into it!

The little guy bobbed up and down, up and down, up and down, as he was being boiled. But he didn't die, he was staring out at them from the pot, he was watching them from the pot.

Earlier on he'd said to them, "Sit around me!" And so they had sat around him. When he thought that everyone was seated, he watched them.

Iyâyâhchipiyitâwât niyâyuw ut-aschîhkuyuw, wiyâuswâpâkâmuwât uyâyuwa ut-âhchâpâskwa. Misiwâ iskwâswâw utâ uyâyîhch; mâmâspinâyichî, iyâsîhkwâyichî.

Tântâ misiwâ iskwâswâw; kiyâ utâ uschîsikuyîhch misiwâ iskwâswâw. Âku wâtitâmistikwânâhwât ut-âhchâpâskwa.

Âku misiwâ nâpâhât.

"Usâ uch," itâw, "ni-wî-mâyâyimikuch," itâw. "Ki-ni-wî-pipikâhikûuchî ut-aschîhkuwâhch," itâw.

Nikitâw, châwât.

Tâkusîhk, mi-wîhtimuwâw umisa.

Then he began to rock their pot. Rock, rock, rock went the pot and, using his bow, he splash-splish-splashed water over them all. He burned them over every inch of their bodies. They suffered terribly, screaming in pain and anger.

He burned every one of them. Their eyes were burned. Then he started beating them over the head with his bow.

And so it was he killed them all!

"They really wanted to have some fun at my expense," he said. "It seems to me they were trying to boil me up good and proper in that pot of theirs!"

He left them behind and went home.

When he got home, he didn't tell his sister what had happened.

3.

Châhkâpâs kiyâ Âchâniskwâw

Chahkapas and Achaniskwaw

3. Châhkâpâs kiyâ Âchâniskwâw

Âku mîn wiyâpiniyich, "Nimisa antâ mâ awânchî ki-mitwâwâskwâhichâtikichî, ki-piskwâhichâtikichî?"

"Âkâ nâsich, Nâsî."

"Michisiyuwa anch ukâwîwa, chiki-nipâhikuyuwa; nipâhâyuwa îyuwa," itikuw.

"Âchâniskwâw. Âchâniskwâw isinikâsuyuwa."

"Âku anch iskwâuch, nîsûch anch, chîyânuw âtâyihtâkusuwâhkw, kwâ-itâyihtâkusich atîhkwa anch muwâuch," itikuw. "Isi-mîchisûuch, isi-nitûwîsûuch," itikuw.

"Âku niyâyuwa ukâwîwa, îyuwa niyâyuwa kwâ-isi-nitûwîsuyichî." itikuw. Mmm. "Mâsâhâyuwa nî ukâwîwa," itikuw. "Nâtâ isâkuyuw antâ wî-chimitâyuwa antâ aschîhch. Âkutâ antâ wiyâpinâyichî nî miyâsâhâyichî ukâwîwa," itikuw. "Âku siyâpwâskusimikuyichî âku nâpâyichî nî."

"Nimisa, mi-nichî-nituwâpimâuch. Chi-kustâchimin â-itâchimit," itâw.

• • •

Âku kâ-wâtâspisust. Âkutâ.

Itâw, "Nimisa," itâw, "michimâ utâ niki-pipâmûhtân," itâw. "Anischikuchâsich niki-nûchîhkuwâuch," itâw. Tâpâ wî-wîhtimuwâw niyâyuw wâ-ihtit.

Wîpich nâtâ kâ-ati-âkuwâskusîhk, nituwâpimâw nâtâ kâ-pâhtuwât kâ-tâyichî.

Âukuw siyâkwâskwâhâhk, piskwâhichâuch anch iskwâuch. Mmm. "Mântâw wâtîhtâhkw," itâw usîma. Niyâtât utâ wâchikâpûstuwât. Wâsusinuwâch, mûchihikûch anch iskwâsich. Mmm.

3. Chahkapas and Achaniskwaw

The following day Chahkapas said to his sister, "Big Sister, who is that, who is it that's making that scraping sound? Who is scraping hides?"

"Don't go near them, Little Brother!"

"Their mother is evil. She'll kill you. She kills people," she said to him.

"Achaniskwaw," she said. "Her name is Achaniskwaw.

"But the two women seem to be like us. They eat caribou. They provide for themselves by eating caribou.

"But their mother, she survives by hunting people!" she said to her little brother. "She wrestles with them," she said, "over there where there's a metal spike sticking up out of the ground. She throws the people she wrestles with onto the spike. They are impaled and die!"

"It's okay, Big Sister," he said. "I won't be able to go near them. You're scaring me with what you're saying."

• • •

Then, the little guy got dressed.

"Big Sister," he said, "I'm going to be wandering around nearby. I'm just going off to hunt squirrels." (He didn't want to tell her what he was actually up to.)

As soon as he was out of sight, hidden behind the trees, he went toward the place where he'd heard the people.

When he emerged from the woods, he found the two young women busy scraping hides. "Ooh, we have a visitor!" the elder one said to her little sister. The older one got up and stood beside Chahkapas. They kept laughing at him. He was amusing to the girls.

• • •

Âku uwâ pîtikimîhch utâ tâw uwâ Âchâniskwâw âsinîhkâtâkinûut.

"Nitânis, châkwân ki-chusinânâwâ?"

"Wîskichân an nusinuwânân nûchîhkim upîwiya," itikuw. Piyâhpuwiyichî antâ. Siyâchuwâpimât, nâtuwâpimât.

Âukunî uyâyuwa.

Siyâchiwâpimât âukuya nâpuwiyichî. Mmm.

"Nitânis, nâpâchikiskw â an?"

"Nâpâchikiskw â?" itikuw. "Âkâ pâchi-iyimuwâ âku," itikuw utânisa. Mi-chistuw. Kwâ-isikâpûwiyichî.

Âku itikuw, "Châstinâs chiki-nipâhikw nikâwînân; nipâhâw nî awâyuwa âti-utîhsîmiyichî nâpâwa," itikuw.

"Nîhî," itâw.

"Nitânis, pîhchâhkw âku, pîhchâhkw."

Mi-wî-pîhchâyuwa utânisa. Mmm. Âku châk, âku itâw an Châhkâpâs, "Pichâwâhkw," itâw. "Niki-pîhchâwân pîhchâwâhkwâ," itâw. Âku pâhchâyichî. Kâ-pîhchâyitwâw utânisa, âku pâhchât Châhkâpâs.

Âku antâ âpit, wâtipimât uyâyuwa iskwâsa.

Âku, mmm, "Châ-asimik mântâw."

• • •

Now then, there was someone inside listening to all of this, and that someone was none other than Achaniskwaw!

"Oh daughters," she called out. "What are you laughing at?" she asked.

"We're laughing at a whisky jack that's fooling around with some caribou fur," they replied. The girls kept on laughing, so Achaniskwaw peeped out at them and then went out to join them.

And there was Chahkapas.

She saw Chahkapas standing there.

"Daughter," she said, "is that a man?"

"Is that a man?" said the daughter, repeating her mother's words. "Don't say another word!" the girl said to her mother. And the mother did as she was told. Chahkapas just stood there.

Now then, the daughter said to Chahkapas, "You can be sure that our mother will kill you for she kills every man that comes our way!"

"I see," said Chahkapas.

"Come now, daughters, get inside," she said to them. "Go on inside," she said.

They didn't want to go inside. Presently, Chahkapas said, "Go on in. I'll go in if you go in." And so the daughters went inside, followed by Chahkapas.

He sat there with the young women.

"Well then," said Achaniskwaw, "I'll feed our visitor."

Âku niyâyuwa îyuwa kâ-muwât, âukuyuwa wâ-itisimât nîstim, âukuyuwa wâ-asimât!

Tântâ chischâyimâw Châhkâpâs nitimikw â-isi-mîchisuyichî. Mi-wî-utinimwâw niyâyuwa âsimikut, pimîyuw âsimikuw; mi-utinimwâw, antâ astâyich.

Âku uch iskwâuch mâyâch uyâyuwa mîchimiyuw âsi-mîchisuch, âukuyuwa mâchiyichî. An Châhkâpâs âsi-mîchisut.

• • •

Âukwâna wâyuwît Âchâniskwâw.

Âukunî uyâyuwa ut-âhchâpîyuwa châmiyâyichî. Wâtinimwât kwâ-ati-kutinimwât. Mmm. "Pimîchikistâw, pimîchikistâw." Mi-sûnimâw ut-âhchâpîyuwa âti-kutinimwât, châmiyimât.

"Nitânis, chiki-pâtûhtâw mâ âku antâ îyuw niki-kutinikw."

"Âkâ wîwî!" Wâ-wîwîwât Châhkâpâs antâ, mâmâhchikunikut. "Âkâ wîwî! Âkâ nâs!" itikuw.

"Mâ âkâ tûtûukw. Niki-nituwâpimâw," itâw. "Châ-wîwîwâkw, misiwâ châ-wîwîwâkw."

"Nîhî," itikuw.

Wâyuwîch, nâtuwâpimâch.

"Âhâk, nitânis! Châ-kutinik îyuw!"

Kâ-itâchimâkinûut itâyimâw, Châhkâpâs. Âku wâwâtinât, miyâsihîkut.

But what she planned to feed him were the remains of a person she'd been eating. That was what she wanted to feed him!

But Chahkapas knew what kinds of things this woman ate, the kinds of things that no one should ever eat. She tried to get him to eat some fat, but he didn't want to take it. He refused it, leaving it where it lay.

But when the young women gave him the food that they ate, he ate that. That was what he had to eat.

• • •

Now then, Achaniskwaw went outside.

Chahkapas's bow was out there, sitting upright where he'd left it. She picked it up and tried to draw back the string. "Yum, yum," she thought. "He's nice and fat! He's nice and fat!" But she couldn't draw the string back on his bow, so she set it back down in its place.

"Daughter," she called out, "that human had better come on out here and challenge me."

"Don't go out!" they told him. Chahkapas wanted to go out but the girls held him tightly. "Don't go out!" they said. "Don't go near her!"

"Let go of me. I'll go out and see what she wants," he said. "Both of you go out. We'll all go outside," he said.

"All right," they replied.

So they all went outside, they went to Achaniskwaw.

"Well now, my daughters!" she said. "I'm going to test this human!"

Chahkapas remembered the story he'd heard about her. He grabbed hold of her and she started to wrestle with him.

Âku niyâyuw isâkuyuw niya kâ-chimitât nâtâ, chimitâw nâtâ isâkuyuw. "Âkutâ antâ châ-wâpinik," itâyimâw. Âkutâ antâ âti-ispitât. Châhkâpâs u, wiyâpâhtâhk niyâyuw isâkuyuw nâtâ, wâhchi-chimitâyich nâtâ; wîyâpâhtimwât. Mmm.

Âti-ûhpitât nî, âkutâ nâtâ ki-wî-wâpinâwâ, kwâ-tuwât. Mi-sâkwâhâw, mi-chî-wâpinâw.

Âku itâw Châhkâpâs niyâyuwa iskwâwa, "Chipâh-mîhtâtâwâw â chikâwîwâw nipâhik?" itâw.

"Nipâhak!" itwâhkâtuwâw uwâ. "Chipâh-châ an tûtuwâw chîhchiwâ kâ-mâsihichât," itâw. "Chipâh-chî-nîhtâ nipâhâw," itâw.

"Nama," itâuch uch iskwâuch, "mi-nipâh-châ-mîhtâtânân âhtuwât mân nâpâwa; âti-wî-wîchimichîhchî, sâs kwâ-nipâhât," itâuch.

Wâchipitimwâch aniyâ mistikuyuw niyâyuw wâtitâmâhwâch ukâwîwa, utâ utischitâniyîhch wâtitâmîstâhwâch. Wâtitâmischitâunâhwâch; utischitâniyîhch ukâwîwa. "Mi-nipâh-châ-mîhtâtânân âhtuwât awâyuwa; wâ-wîchimîhchitwâwî nâpâwa nâpâhât," itikuw utânisa.

"Nitânis! Âkâ pitimâ tûtûukw! Kâpit tûtûukw!" itâw.

Miyâsâhât an Châhkâpâs.

Wâpâhtimwâw tântâ Châhkâpâs niyâyuwa ut-isâkumiyuw nâtâ wâ-wâpinikut, nâyâ châmitâyichî nâtâ.

Âkutâ antâ âti-ispitât. Wâtinât uyâyuwa, uyâyuwa miyâsihîkut uyâyuwa Âchâniskwâwa Châhkâpâs. Âku utâ wâhchi-pistinât usûkiniyîhch; âkutâ utâ wâhchi-sâpusimât utâ usûkiniyîhch, wâhchi-sâpuchiniyichî.

The metal spike was sticking up out of the ground. She'd put it there. "I'll impale him on that," she thought, pulling him over toward it. Chahkapas realized what she was doing, seeing the spike sticking up from the ground.

She started to lift him up and tried to throw him right onto the spike. But she was no match for him, and she couldn't get him onto it.

Then Chahkapas said to the young women, "Would you miss your mother if I killed her?"

"Kill her!?" Achaniskwaw yelled back at him. "You won't be able to do it," she said. "Achaniskwaw can really fight!" she said. "You'll never be able to kill her!"

"No," said the girls, "we wouldn't miss her because of what she does to men! Whenever we want to marry a man, she kills him!"

So they grabbed a stick and hit their mother over and over again on the calves of her legs. They hit her repeatedly on her calves. "We wouldn't miss her because of the way she treats people! Whenever we want to marry a man, she kills him!" they told Chahkapas.

"Daughters! Don't do this to me! Don't do this to me!" she said.

Chahkapas fought with her.

He saw her metal spike sticking up. That's where she wanted to throw him. She'd put it there herself for just that purpose!

And that's the spot that he dragged her to. He held on to her as she wrestled with him and he dropped her ass-first onto the spike. It ran her through, all the way from her ass right through the middle.

Kwâ-itipit, mi-chî-âhchîw, mi-chî-âhchistim ut-isâkum. Mmm.

Âku itâw Châhkâpâs, "Chi-mîhtâtâwâw â chikâwîwâw?" itâw.

Mmm. "Nama," itikuw, "mi-ni-mîhtâtânân," itikuw. Wâchipitimiyichî mistikuyuw wâtitâmâhamiyichî ustikwân.

Âukwâyâ, nâpâhikut utânisa.

• • •

Âku itâw Châhkâpâs, "Nimis antâ tâw," itâw. "Chipâh-nituwâpimâwâw, chipâh-wîchâunâw; âku chipâh-tâpituwînânuw, chipâh-kinuwâyimikuwâw," itâw.

"Nîhî," itikuw. Châtûhtâch, nâtuwâpimâch.

Mmm. Piyâchi-tikusîhk, "Nimisa, ni-pâsuwâuch uch chiwîchâwâkinich châ-sîtwâyimitwâw," itâw umisa. Utâ wâhchi-sâchiwâpiyîchî âukw uyâ nâpuwiyichî iskwâwa nîsîyuwa.

"Nâsî," itikuw, "pispinâ chi-nipâhimâchânî ukâwîwa?"

"Ni-nipâhimâwâ niy," itâw, "ni-wî-mâyâyimikuyuwa," itâw. Pâhchât Châhkâpâs, kwâ-isikâpûuch anch iskwâuch. "Nimisa," itâw, "pîhtâtisâhuch," itâw. Âku an iskwâw âyûhtâpitâhk. "Pîhchâkw," itâw, "pâhtûhtâkw," itâw.

Pâhchâyichî, pâhtikâhât.

Âku châk wâchimâst âku. Âku â-ihtât.

And there she sat, unable to move. She couldn't move the metal spike.

Now, Chahkapas said, "Do you miss your mother?"

"No," they replied. "We don't miss her," they said. They grabbed a stick and kept beating her about the head with it.

And that was that! Her daughters killed her.

• • •

Then Chahkapas said to them, "My older sister lives over there a way. You should go see her. You should come along with me so that we can be together. She could take care of you," he said.

"All right," they replied. And off they went to see her.

When Chahkapas got back home, he said to his sister, "Big Sister, I've brought you some company." His sister took a peek outside and saw the two young women standing there.

"Little Brother," she said, "you didn't kill their mother, did you?"

"I did," he said. "She was very disrespectful to me." Chahkapas went inside, but the young women remained standing outside. "Big Sister," he said, "ask them in." Then she opened the door and said to the girls, "Come in. Come this way."

And so they came in, she let them in.

And that little guy, Chahkapas, lived with them. He stayed right there, never going far from them.

4.

Châhkâpâs kiyâ Michi-îyûch

Chahkapas and the Bad People

4. Châhkâpâs kiyâ Michi-îyûch

Wiyâpiniyich mîn, piyâhtuwât awâyuwa antâ; pâkwâhichâwiyichî miskumîhch. Mistimiskwa nûchîhkawâyuwa. Piyâhtuwât mâtwâsikutâhichâyichî.

Mmm. “Nimisa, awânchî mânâtâ ki-mitwâsikutâhichâtikichî antâ?”

“Âkâ tûtûuch Nâsî, âkâwîy nituwâpimich; mistimiskwa anch nûchîhkuwâuch. Utinimiskwâhâuch îyuwa wâtîhtikutwâwî, âku pâkistuwâpitikuyichî mistimiskwa, âku wâsinuwâch.”

“Nîhî,” itâw.

“Michi-îyûch anch.” Mmm.

Wâwâtâspisut. Mmm.

“Nimisa,” itâw, “niki-nânituwâpimâuch mâ anischikuchâsich,” itâw. “Niki-nûchîhkuwâuch,” itâw.

Mmm. Wîpich kâ-ati-âkuwâskusîhk, âkutâ âti-stûhtât antâ nâtuwâpimât; pâhtuwâw antâ tântâ mâtwâsikutâhichâyichî.

• • •

Âukunî uyâyuwa kâ-nûchîhkuwâyichî mistimiskwa, pikwâyichâyuwa.

“Mmm. Mântâw wâtîhtâhkw, mântâw.” Sâs chî-chipâhwâuch uch utâ wîstiyîhch, amiskwa mistimiskwa. “Utinimiskwâhîhkw,” itâuch.

Sâs kîpwâ kâ-pâhtuwât umisa kâ-itâchimâyichî. Mmm.

“Utinimiskwâh, nitwâkiminich; sâs ûhchi-chî-chipâhwâkinûuch,” itâuch. Mmm.

4. Chahkapas and the Bad People

Again, the following day, he heard someone nearby chopping a hole in the ice. They were busy looking for giant beaver. He could hear them breaking the ice.

"Big Sister," he said, "who are those people over there who are chopping a hole in the ice?"

"Don't bother with them, Little Brother!" she replied. "Don't go near them! They're hunting giant beaver," she said. "They make anyone they meet go after beaver and then the giant beaver pulls him into the water, and everyone has a laugh at him!"

"I see," said Chahkapas.

"They're bad people," she said.

He got himself dressed.

"Big Sister," he said, "I'm going to look for squirrels. I'm going to be busy doing that."

As soon as he was out of sight, hidden behind the trees, he set off to find the bad people. He heard them breaking ice.

• • •

They were the ones who were making a hole in the ice to go after giant beaver.

"Oh, a visitor! We have a visitor!" they said, seeing him coming. They had already closed the giant beaver up inside its lodge. "Make him go after the beaver," they said.

Of course, he'd already heard about these people from his sister!

"Come on, go after the beaver!" they said. "Put your hand in and feel around for it's already sealed up inside the lodge."

Kwâ-ati-pîhtâyâkunichipiyihusit chikisâm. Nâtwâkiminât niyâyuwa amiskwa, nâtâ nâtwâkiminichât.

Nâham uyâyuw usuyuw uyâyuwa âskwâyich uyâyuw usuyuw, âkutâ utâ wâhchisichinât wâhchi-ûchipitât. Âku uyâyuwa, ut-âhchâpiya; ut-âhchâpâskwa uyâyuwa mi-pistinâw ut-âhchâpâskwa. Âukunî wâhchi-pistinât wâhchi-utâmistikwânâhwât antâ â-wâpinât.

Mîn nâtwâkiminichât, mîn wâhchi-utinât kutika. Iyâpich kwâ-tuwât; wâtitâmistikwânâhwât antâ â-wâpinât, nîsîyuwa.

Âku uyâyuwa ut-âhchâpâtuy, ut-âhchâpâskwa mânât ut-âhchâpâtuy, nâswâpîhkâtât niyâyuwa ut-amiskuma, sâkâpitât pwâstûutât. Âhâ, châtûhtât.

• • •

"Âku tân âhtit an âku? Ki-chîtûutâwâ chit-amiskuminuwa. Nâtîhkw! Minimîhkw!" itâkinûuch anch uschinîchisûch.

Niyâtâch, iyâyituw utâ ûhchi-pimûhtâyuwa. Wâwâch ki-apisîsuwâ, ki-mimâhkisâmâsuwâ kwâ-isinâkusit. Mmm.

"Iyâukw, iyâukw. Châtûutânîkw."

"Châkwân wâhchi-utinitwâw nit-amiskuminânch? Pâsûuch!" itikuw. Mmm.

"Châkwân wâhchi-utinitwâw?" itikukw, "Pâsûuch!" itikuw.

"Châtûutânîkw, châtûutânîkw. Îtuw utâ ûhchi-utinîhkuch."

Âku utâ îtuw wâhchi-utinâyichî.

Now then, that little guy, still wearing his snowshoes, dove right into the snow. He felt around in the water for the beaver, he searched all around him with his hands.

He caught it by the end of its tail and pulled it out. He was still holding on to his bow—he hadn't let go of his bowshaft. He let go of the beaver, hit it on the head with the bow, and threw it aside.

One more time, he felt around in the water, and he caught another beaver in the same spot. He did the same thing with this beaver, hitting it on the head with his bow and throwing it aside.

Then he took the string off his bow, tied the two beavers together with it, securing the bundle to him by wrapping the remaining line around his shoulders. And off he went.

• • •

Now then, the people wondered, "What is he doing? He seems to be carrying off our beavers!" They shouted to their young men, "Go after him! Get those beavers back!"

The young men caught up to Chahkapas, walking along either side of him. Although he seemed to be small, his snowshoes looked big.

"Help me. Help me," he said to them. "Take this load off my back."

"Why did you take our beavers?" the young men asked. "Bring them here! Why did you take them?"

"Take this load off my back," he replied. "Take it off my back. Get them both off my back."

The young men did as he asked, taking the load off both sides of his back.

Pîmâhkunâpitâsit uyâyuwa pâikw, mîn kutichiyuw. Âku mi-chî-âhchipîhtâyuwa tântâ utâ pipâsichinimwâw utâ utîhchîyuwa, pipîmâhkunâpitâw. Mîn kutika. Âku mi-chî-wiyâs tûtâkuw, tântâ utâ pipîmâhkunâpitâw pipâsikwâpinâpitâw.

Châwâyichî. Mmm.

"Wâpâhtim âsinâkwâhimîht! Nit-ati-wî-châtûutânânân chit-amiskuminuwa niyâhkâ châmutit. Wâpihtim â-tûtâhk."

Miyitâw itimutâwâw utîhchîyuwa.

"Nituwâpimâtâw! Nituwâpimâtâw!" itâuch. "Châ-wî-tipâhamâsuwâhkw. Nituwâpimâtâw!"

• • •

Âku uyâyuwa umisa tâkusûhutât uyâyuwa amiskwa, kwâ-ati-pâhkunâyichî. Kwâ-itisumât tântâ, kwâ-ati-pikistuwâwât ut-aschîhkûhch utâ. Mmm. Âku uyâyuwa utî-usimiskwâh uyâyuwa. "Nimisa, âku akwânich," itâw, "châ-mwâmiskwâyâhkw," itâw.

Âku niya kûna niyâtâyichî umisa, châhchinâyichî kûna, piyâtuwâyichî awâyuwa piyâtwâtimiyichî.

"Nâsî," itikuw, "pâtwâtimuch awânchî," itikuw. "Pispinâ ûhch chiki-châmutinâchâ uch amiskuch?" itikuw.

Mmm. "Nimisa, nûtinimiskwâhîkuch uyâyuwa. Kâkiyâ nutimiskumîhkâkuch nit-itâyimâuch. Nimisa, pâsûuch nitâsimich, nitâsimich pâsûuch.

Chî-kinuwâyihtim misiwâ châkwâniyuw. Mâyikut. Antâ â-wâpinât tistuwâhîkinich wâhkwâsâkâyich wîch âku antâ tâmîhch â-tât.

Suddenly, the little guy grabbed one of them by the wrist and gave it a sharp twist backwards. He broke the wrist, so that the young man couldn't move his hand anymore. He did the same thing to the other man. Neither of them could do anything because Chahkapas had twisted their hands back and broken their wrists.

They ran back home.

"Look what he did to us!" they said. "We were trying to get back those beavers that he stole, and look what he did to us!"

He had bent their hands so that they were now attached in exactly the opposite direction from what is normal.

"Let's go and look for him! Let's go and look for him!" they all shouted. "Let's try and pay him back for this. Let's go and look for him!"

• • •

Now then, Chahkapas arrived back home to his sister, still carrying the beavers on his back. He told her to skin them for him, and then he dropped them into her pot of water. And as the beavers were boiling, he said to his sister, "Big Sister, take them off the fire. Let's scoop out the meat and eat some beaver."

When his sister went out to get some snow, while she was running off to get snow, she heard someone coming toward them.

"Little Brother," she said, "I hear people coming our way. You didn't steal these beaver, did you?" she asked.

"Big Sister, they made me go after these beaver. I thought they must have killed them for me. Big Sister, bring me my conjuring tools. My conjuring tools, bring them to me."

Wâtîhtâch uch îyûch niyâyuwa mîchîwâpiyuw. Mi-chischâyihtimuch châ-ûhchi-pîhchâch, wîhkwâsâkâyuw tântâ. Kâ-ati-utitâmâhamuchî kwâ-tutâhch. Mi-chischâyihtimuch tântâ châ-ûhchi-pîhchâch. Mmm.

Âku utâ âhtâsûut utâ pîhtikimîhch.

"Nimisa, akwânich âku chit-amiskuminuch, kischûchânichî. Âku châ-mwâmiskwâyâhkw." Wî-pipâhtâwâyimusuw, wiyâyuwa îyuwa utâ atâyichî wîwîtimîhch. Mi-chî-wiyâstûtâhkuw, mi-chî-pîhtikwâkuw, kiyâ mi-chî-pikwâhamiyuwa wîch âsinâkuniyich, wîhkwâsâkâyuw tântâ. Mmm.

Âku itâuch, "Âkâ pimâhimâtâw," itâuch, "Nâkitâtâw," itâuch. "Âskw châ-wîhkiyâsâhkw âkâ itâyihtâhchâ utâ. Âskw châ-wîhkiyâsâhkw," itâuch. Mmm.

Nâkitikut. Mmm. Âku miyâmiskwâst, âkwânât ut-amiskuma. Âku kâ-chîsi-mîchisutwâw, âku mîn wâtinât niyâyuwa utâsima kâ-isinâkuniyich, mîn âsinâkuniyich wîch.

He kept all kinds of things, and it was these that she gave to him. He threw them up into the air, up to the top of the tent where the tent poles cross, and their tent turned into stone, and they were still inside it.

The young men reached the tent, but they didn't know how to get in because it had turned to stone. Trying to find a way in, they banged on it over and over with their fists. But they still couldn't find a way in.

The little guy was in there, in the tent.

"Big Sister," he said, "take our beavers off the fire. They must be done by now. Let's eat beaver." He wanted the people outside to hear him. They couldn't hurt him, they couldn't reach him inside the tent. Nor were they able to do any damage to his house because it was made of stone.

"Let's not bother with him," they said. "Let's leave him here. Later, we'll trick him. Later, when he's not expecting it, we'll trick him."

And so they took off, leaving him behind, and little Chahkapas took his beaver off the fire and ate it. After they had finished eating, again he took up his conjuring tools and turned the tent back into what it had been before.

5.

Châhkâpâs Mâmîhkutîhchikisuw Kâ-kûhchipihîkut

Chahkapas Swallowed by a Fish

5. Châhkâpâs Mâmîhkutîhchikisuw Kâ-kûhchipihîkut

Âku nâpiniyich, âku utî-ihtâh nâpiniyich. Âku asuch wâchich nipîhch.

Âku itâw ana usîma, "Nâsî," itâw, "châ-âkâ-nîhtâ antâ nipîhch pimuchâyin chikiskw," itâw. "Tâw antâ nimâs mâsitit antâ nipîhch," itâw. "Kwâstâtikusît," itâw, "chiki-nipâhikw," itâw.

Mmm. "Nîhî, nîhî," itâw umisa. (Tâpâ châskâ niskumâw âti-itâchî, tâpâ titâpwâtuwâw umisa.)

Mmm. "Nimisa," itâw. Châtutât, "Nimisa," itâw, "kuschâ mâ," itâw. "Chîhchiwâ ni-wî-muwâw nimâs," itâw. "Kuschâ," itâw, "wâpinikuschâ," itâw. "Âku an chit-âpitâsîhtâkinâskw an," itâw, "niyâyuwa utâpitâsîhtâniyuw, mistikw antâ wâs chimitâkinûw, âkutâ antâ châ-ûhchi-sikâpitimin an chikuskin," itâw.

Tâpâkâ ninâhitâkuw umisa â-itisumâchî, wiyâpinikuschâyichî. Âku uyâyuwa mistikuyuw châmitâyichî uyâyuwa âkutâ; utâ miyâkupitimiyichî âku nâtâ âtâpâkistâyichî ukuskin.

Âku nâtâ pâpâmûhtât. Châk utî-pipâmûhtâh, pâmuchât nâtâ ukiskwa nipîhch. Âkûhchiniyichî ukiskwa. "Niki-nâtâhwâw," itâyimâw ukiskwa. Niyâtâhwâst niyâyuwa ukiskwa. Mmm.

"Mâmîhkutîhchikisuw niki-wâukimikw!
Mâmîhkutîhchikisuw niki-wâukimikw!"

isitâsuw.

Piyâhtâkut, niyâtâhukut. "Âukuw uwâ pâmiskâst," awânis u âku itikuw, "apisîsuw â-ihtichî." Kwâ-chipiyihîkut, miyâkumikut.

5. Chahkapas Swallowed by a Fish

Now then, the summertime had come and they were living along the shore of a lake.

"Little Brother," his sister said, "you should never fire your arrow into the water! There's a big fish there in that water. It's dangerous," she said. "It'll kill you!" she said.

"Okay, okay," he replied. (Most likely, he was just going along with his sister while in fact having no intention of paying any heed to her advice.)

"Big Sister!" he said. He called out to her, "Big Sister, you have to go fishing! I really feel like eating some fish," he said. "Go on, go fishing! Set a hook in the water overnight," he said. "You see your doorpost, that pole you have set upright there to use for your door? Tie your fishing line to that."

Naturally, since his sister always did everything he ordered her to do, she went off to set an overnight line in the water. She tied the line to her doorpost pole and laid the line out in the water.

Now then, Chahkapas was walking around close to where the line was set. Suddenly, while he was walking, he fired an arrow into the water. It landed on the water and floated there on the surface. "I'll swim out toward my arrow," he thought to himself. And then the little guy swam out to his arrow.

"A big red-finned fish will swallow me whole!
A big red-finned fish will swallow me whole!"

was what he sang.

The fish heard him and swam toward him. "What a little swimmer we have here!" said the fish. "He's very small to be doing what he's doing!" Then, biting him, the fish began to swallow him!

"Âhâhâ!" itâw. "Âkâ mâkumî!" itâw. "Nûtimikûchipiyihî!" itâw.

Mi-mâkumikuw, kwâ-ati-kûchipiyihîkut.

"Âhâ!" itâw. "Âkâ ispihî nâtâ â-wî-kwâtiyâyin," itâw, "sâchiskwâsimî," itâw.

Âku utâ wâhchi-sâskwâsimikut utâ, utâ utûnîhch wâhchi-sâchiskwâsinist nâtâ antâ utûnîhch.

"Utâ nâtâ mâ âti-ispiyi," itâw, "nâtâ," itâw, utâ umisa kâ-itâyihtimwât ukuskiniyuw. Âkutâ âti-ispiyiyichî tâpwâ, nâtuwâpâtimwât umisa ukuskiniyuw wiyâpâhtâhk âstâyich umisa ukuskiniyuw.

Itâw, "Aniyâ mâ antâ châkwân kistâwâ," itâw. "Chîwâpiyî mâ." itâw. Âku mîn châwâpiyichî.

Wiyâpâhtimwât utâ, mân kistâwâ châkwân. "Nâtâha," itâw. Niyâtâhamiyichî.

"Utâtah," itâw. Wâtâhtimiyichî.

Sâs mikw mustinimwâw, mustinimwâw kuskiniyuw, mâmâhchikunimwât, mâmâhchikunimuwât kîpwâ iyâhchistimiyichî niyâyuwa ukuskiniyuw umisa. Âku uyâyuw kâ-uhchikâpitimiyichî uyâyuw pîhtikimîhch uyâyuw wîchiyîhch. Iyâyâchipitimiyichî uyâyuwa umistikumiyuwa. Châschâyimât nûchîhkimiyichî ukuskin uwâ iskwâw nâtuwâpimât.

Niyânâskânât. Âkwâstâpât mâmîhkutîhchikisuwa. Nâpâhât. Wâtinât châwâtâhât.

"Âkutâ Nimis châ-iyâyuwit châstinâs châ-piskisut, châ-piskiswât unimâsima."

"Ahaha!" said Chahkapas. "Don't bite me! Swallow me whole!"

And the fish stopped biting him and began to swallow him whole.

"Ahaha!" said Chahkapas. "Don't swallow me completely! Leave my head sticking out!"

And the fish let the little guy's head stick out of its mouth, let Chahkapas lie there with his head sticking out of the fish's mouth.

Then, pointing to the place where he thought his sister's hook was, he said to the fish, "Swim over there." And sure enough, as the fish swam toward that spot, Chahkapas searched for and found where his sister's hook was set.

"It looks like there's something over there," he said to the fish. "Swim back so we can see." So the fish swims back again.

Now then, Chahkapas saw where the hook was set and said to the fish, "Swim towards that."

"Take it into your mouth," he told the fish. And the fish swallowed the hook.

Chahkapas already had a hold of the line. He held on and on, holding tight as the fish struggled against his sister's hook. She had tied the other end of the line to the doorpost of her tent. Seeing the pole move, she realized there was a fish struggling on her hook and she ran out to check her line.

Hand over hand she hauled in her line. She dragged the big red-finned fish out of the water. She killed it, picked it up, and took it home.

Chahkapas (still inside the fish) thought to himself, "My sister will finish me off, for sure. She'll rip me open when she guts the fish."

Pâskiswâyichî uyâyuwa nimâsa. Âku pâtus iyâhchît, nâsch nâtâ nâtâ nimâsa âsinâkusit, nâsch nâtâ â-wîhkwâsît niyâyuwa nimâs âsinâkusit utiya. Âkutâ antâ âspiyuhust, âkutâ nâtâ âtâwât. Âku wiyâyuw châ-misimiyichî utâ miyâtisimiyichî.

Âku nâtâ âspitimiyichî utâyuw uschiwâyîhch wâhchi-wîwîpiyihust!

"Tâpwâ wâsâ Nimisa ni-wîhchâkitiyâmikw," itâw. "Ni-wîhchâkitiyâmikw chîhchiwâ," itâw.

"Wâsâ usâm!" itikuw. "Âkâ chî-îpwâhkânâwâ." itikuw. "Mâ chi-pâhtûun châ-âkâ-nîhtâ pimuchâyin nipîhch antâ pâmuchâyin chikiskw kâ-itân?" itikuw.

"Pispinâ chi-musâwânâchâ?" itikuw. "Chipâh-nipâhikw âku chi-kûhchipiyikuchâ."

Mi-chî-nipâhikuw iyâpich. Mmm.

Âku â-ihtât mîn antâ.

Now then, as she began to cut the big fish open, the little guy moved himself back into the deepest part of the fish's stomach. He retreated to the part of the stomach that looks like a bag, to the part that looks like a bag. That's where he moved himself to, and that's where he stayed! She sliced off a piece of the stomach as she was cutting into the fish.

And as she moved toward the stomach with her knife, out jumped the little fellow!

"Oh dear," he said. "The fish has made me very fishy-smelly! It has really left me smelling bad!"

"For goodness sake!" she said. "You're not very smart, are you! Didn't you hear me when I told you never to fire an arrow into the water?

"You just had to go into the water, didn't you? It could have killed you. It could have swallowed you!"

But it didn't kill him.

And there he stayed, at that same place by the shore of the lake.

6.

Utinâkinûyuwa Châhkâpâs Umisa

Chahkapas's Sister Is Taken

6. Utinâkinûyuwa Châhkâpâs Umisa

Âku châk utî-pipâmûhtâh mîn, âkutât ukiskwa mistikûhch. Niyâtâtuwâmutuwât. Âku wâtîhtâchî ukiskwa, âku pûtâtât niyâyuwa mistikwa, âku mîn âti-chinwâskusiyichî, âskiyâskw.

Châk chîhchiwâ kwâ-chinwâskusiyichî, châk nâtâ kwâ-utîhtât pîsimwa.

Antâ âhtâyichî aschiy chipâh-itâyihtâkuniyuw. Âku antâ wiyâpâhtâhk âsinâkuniyich, pâpâmûhtât antâ, anischikuchâsa âukunî âhtâyichî.

Âku uyâyuwa pîsimwa â-pimûhtâyichî umâskinâyuw, âukuyuw wiyâpâhtimwât. Chîhchiwâ miywâyuw niyâyuw aschîyuw mâskâhk. Châwât.

Wâsîhtât antâ nî antâ "Nipâh-nipânân," âtâyihtâhk. Nistwâw isinâkûhtâw wâchistinîhchât antâ chipâh-nipâuch nîst niyâyuwa umisa.

Âku uyâyuwa âkâ ihtât uyâyuwa, uyâyuwa âkâ ihtât, niyâtâhukuyichî michi-îyuwa umisa, wâtinâyichî, mânâyichî.

Âukuyuwa tâpâhamâsuyichî kâ-kichâmutimât ut-amiskumiyuwa châtâhuyâyichî. Âku wîwa mi-pimâhimâyuwa, umisa mikw mânâkinuyichî.

Tâkusîhk. Mmm.

Âku itâw, "Nimis aniyâ, tân âhtit?" itâw.

Mmm. "Tâpâ tâw uyâ chimis," itikuw. "Wâs aniyâhkâ nutîhtâhukunânich îyûch. Minâhuyâuch niyâhkâ chimisa," itikuw. "Mâniyâyitâ âskâpimichîhch," itikuw, "nâham âschimâch," itikuw.

6. Chahkapas's Sister Is Taken

Now then, while Chahkapas was wandering around, wandering here and there, he climbed up a tree to get an arrow of his that he'd left hanging there. When he reached the arrow, he blew on the tree and it began to grow taller and taller and taller.

All of a sudden it was so tall it reached the sun.

The tree had grown so tall, it had reached a place where there seemed to be land. And as Chahkapas walked all around, exploring this new land, he saw that there were squirrels there.

He also saw the path the sun takes as it travels across the sky each day. He'd found a truly beautiful land up there. Then he went back home.

He had made himself a place to sleep there. "We'll need a place to sleep," he said to himself. So he had fixed them up some little nests for sleeping. He had made them nests in three different places.

But while he was gone, while he was away from his sister, those bad people from whom he had once stolen beavers, they came along and kidnapped her.

They took her away by canoe as a punishment for stealing their beavers. It was just Chahkapas's sister that they paddled away with—they didn't take his wives.

Chahkapas arrived home.

"Where's my sister?" he said. "What has happened to her?"

"Your sister isn't here," his wives replied. "They came by canoe, and they carried her off!" They pointed to the place where they'd last seen her. "That's where we last saw them," they said. "They were heading in that direction in their canoe."

Mâmîchisuhkâhikut wîwa kâ-mîchisuch. Âku itâw, "Niki-nituwâpimâw nimis," itâw, "niki-nituwâpimâw," itâw. Kwâ-ati-wîwît mikw ut-âhchâpîsa tâhkunâw, tâhkunâw ut-âhchâpîya.

Niyâsipât mwâsâskupâtâst. Ustipâch pimipâhtâsuw, tâpâ ut uwtuw muyâm â pimiskupâhtâst, kwâ itit. Siskâhupâhtâsuw utâ ut-âhchâpîya.

Âukwâyâ mâskûtiyichî ki-sunâskwâtâmwâ îyuw kwâ-itist utî-pimipâhtâsîh ustipâch. Ki-sunisunâskwâtâsuwâ isinuwâuch unâpâmisuwâwa. Âukwâna âskwâpimâch.

Nâtâ mâk wâtîhchipitât utâ umisa âhtâyichî. Kwâ-ati-pîhchât mîchiwâhpiyuw. Kwâ-ati-nâtât umisa, tâpâ unâyimâw antâ âhtâyichî umisa, wâtinât umisa, kwâ-ati-wîwîtâhât, wânînât.

Tâpâ chischiyuwa umisa, mi-chischiyuwa, kwâ-ati-utinât sîtutîhkwâmâsuw tâpâkâ sâpisuw chîhchiwâ, kwâ-ati-wîwîtâhât.

Nâtâ mâk kâ-ati-nâtâ nâsipâtâhât. Âkutâ wâyâsitûtuwât umisa. Mikw ki-pûpûtâtâsuwâ kwâ-tûtuwât umisa, sâs kwâ-îpwâhkâyichî. Kwâ-ati-chîhchipâhtât, âti-chîhchipâhtât.

"Tân âhtiyâkw u âkâ wiyâsitûtuwâkw?" itâuch uch îyûch tâpâkâ mîhchâtûch. Nûchîhkuwâch.

Pipîhpimwâuch niyâyuwa akitâskwa, niyâyuw pipîhpimuwâuch utî-ati-pimipâhtâsîh. Ninâutinisuw niyâyuwa akitâskwa pipîhpimuwâw. Mikw châkwâniyuw âsi-utîhchinâhk an kwâ-isi-nipâhât niyâyuwa.

After they themselves had finished eating, his wives gave him a good meal. Then he said to them, "I'm going to look for my sister." He said, "I'm going to look for her." He went outside, taking only his little bow, he took his bow.

Going down to the shore, he ran out across the surface of the water as if it were ice. That little guy ran across the top of the water, he had no canoe, and it was as if he were running on ice! He ran along carrying his bow.

It was like he was skating over a frozen lake, seeing him run there across the surface of the water. The women looked out and saw their little husband on the water, looking as if he was skating around on ice. And there he went, he vanished from sight.

He reached the place where his sister was, and he went inside the house that was there. Knowing exactly where she was, he went over to her and picked her up to take her outside and try to rouse her.

But she could not be roused, she was unconscious. But the little guy, because he was so strong, was able to carry her under his arm. He carried her outside.

He took her down to the shore, where he did some magic to help her. He blew on her. He blew and blew, until, all of a sudden, she came to. Then he started to run away. He started to run away.

"Why don't you use magic against him?" the bad people asked the kidnappers. There were lots of them and only one of him! They had to do something to sort him out!

As he was running, they started throwing axes after him. But the little guy just caught the axes in mid-air and threw them right back! He just grabbed whatever he could reach and used it to kill them.

"Âkâ tûtuwîhkw, âkâ tûtuwîhkw," itâuch anch chisâîyûch, "Chiki-nipâhikuwâw," itâuch. "Chîhchiwâ sâs chi-misti-nipâhikuwâw," itâuch. "Âkâ nûchihîkuwîhkw," itâuch.

• • •

Âukwânâ mwâsâskupâhtâsiyichî nipîhch ustipâch pimipâhtâsuw. Âku utî-pimipâyitûhtâw, umisa utâ ustâhkunikuw uspiskunîhch, antâ wâstâhkunikut, wâstâhkunikut antâ uspiskunîhch.

"Tântâ kwâ-ihtât, âkutâ antâ wîs-tâhkunî," itâw. "Mikw â-isinûyin âkun châ-itiyin," itâw.

Kwâ-îyuyichî ut-awâsimiyuwa utî-pimipâyitûhtâw, sâs ut-awâsîmîhkuwâkinûyuwa châpî-nîhtâuchiyichî utîhkutimisa.

"Nimisa, âkâ-iyipîhchâtâ mâ âkus chipâh-mikuskâchîhkuwâuch nîsîyuwa nîhtâuchiyichî. Chipâh-mîhchâtûuch sûk usâm chiyipi-nîhtâuchûuch."

Wâtâmistikwânâhwâst wiyâpinâst. Âukun mikw âhtûtuwât wâtâmistikwânâhwât nî wiyâpinât nâtâ. Misiwâ îyuyichî âukw mi-chiskâkuyuwa umisa.

Tâkusitâhât umisa wîchiwâhch.

Their Elders said to those people, “You’d better stop messing with him. Leave him alone! He’ll kill you. Indeed, he has already killed many of you! Leave him alone!”

• • •

And there he went, the little guy, running into the water, running on the surface of the water. The two of them, him and his sister, running with her holding tight onto his back. She held tight onto his back as they ran.

“Hold on tight onto my back!” he told his sister. “And do whatever I do.”

But as they ran, she was giving birth to children. She was having babies as they were running, for she had already been made pregnant. And even as they were running, Chahkapas’s nephews were growing up fast.

“Big Sister,” he said, “you mustn’t let these children live. When they grow up, they’ll make trouble for generations to come. Don’t let them grow up! Because they’re growing up so fast, there could end up being lots and lots of them.”

And so the little guy hit them on the head and threw them aside. That is what he did. He hit them on the head and threw them aside. By this time they had all been born, there were none left in his sister’s belly.

Finally, Chahkapas arrived home with his sister.

7.

Châhkâpâs Kâ-tâpikwâtât Pîsimwa

Chahkapas Snares the Sun

7. Châhkâpâs Kâ-tâpikwâtât Pîsimwa

"Nimisa," itâw, "âku mâ châ-stûhtâyâhkw, châ-chîhtisimâhkuch awânchî usâm chî-mikuskâchihkâkunûch," itâw, "utâ âtâyâhkw," itâw. "Ni-miskân antâ aschiy châ-itûhtâyâhkw," itâw.

"Nîhî," itikuw. Wiyâpiniyich châtûhtâch.

"Âhâk Nimisa, âukuw châ-ûhchi-sâkichuwâyâhkw u mistikw," itâw. Wâhchi-sâkichuwâyichî uyâyuwa wîwa kiyâ uyâyuwa umisa.

Âku utâ wîy utâhch, utâ utâhch, utâ âkutâ wâhchi-pimûhtâst. Âku an châskwâyâpimuyitwâwî, âku piyâschiniyichî antâ antâ antâ iyâmipiyichî kîpwâ, châskwâyâpimuyichî kîpwâ. Wâhchi-nûtinâst, âku mîn pâstinâst, âku mîn âti-stûhtâyichî. Utâhch utâ ûhchi-pimûhtâsuw.

Nistwâw, nistwâw nipâuch, nistwâw tipiskâyuw antâ âti-pimûhtâch, antâ âspisâyich wâ-itûhtâch. Âku wâtîhtâhch, tâkusîhch niyâyuwa kâ-miskâhk aschîyuw. Mmm. Âkutâ âhtâch.

"Nimisa, âukw âku ni-miskân aschiy kâ-itân," itâw.

"Nîhî," itikuw, "tâpwâ miywâw," itikuw. Âkutâ âhtâch.

• • •

Âku châk nûchîhkuwât niyâyuwa pîsimwa, mi-chî-wâpimâw antâ â-pimûhtâyichî. Âti antâ nî chipiskinâhch ihtâw, âku an piyâchi-pâsunâkusiyichî, âku nâpât nî.

7. Chahkapas Snares the Sun

"Big Sister," said Chahkapas, "let's leave! Let's run away from all these people here. There's too much trouble going on around here right now. I have found a land away over there where we can go."

"All right," she said. And the very next day they set off.

"Now then, Big Sister," he said, "we're going to climb this tree." And up the tree they all went, his wives, his older sister, and Chahkapas himself.

He himself was right there behind them all. And as the women became dizzy and slipped off the tree (it was only natural that they would feel a little dizzy and fall), he caught them and set them back down so that they could start out anew. And all the time the little guy walked at the back.

Three times, three times they slept. Three times on their journey night fell on them as they walked their allotted distance for the day. And in this way they reached the land that Chahkapas had found. They arrived, and that is where they stayed.

"Big Sister," said Chahkapas, "this is the land I told you I had found."

"Yes," she replied. "It's very beautiful." And that is where they stayed.

• • •

Now then, at a certain point in time, Chahkapas became curious about the sun because he couldn't see the path along which it travelled. Every time he reached the end of the sun's

Âku pâmûhtâyikwânî wâmâskâkut. Sâs chî-pimûhtâyisipinî âti-pâkupiyichî. Mi-chî-wâpimâw.

"Awâchâ âku?" itâyimâw.

"Niki-tâpikwâtâw, niki-wî-wâpimâw," itâyimâw. "Âhâk, Nimisa." Nâtuwâpimât. "Nimisa," itâw, "pâtâh antâ sistikw," itâw. "Niki-âpichîhtân," itâw. Mmm. Âku mâyikut kîpwâ sistikuyuw âsinîhkâṭâhk, âukuyuwa mâyikut.

Tâpâkâ misîhtâw, chinwâpâchîhtâw niyâyuwa wâsîhtât aniyâ sistikuyuw. Pûpûhtâtâhk châchî sûhkâpâkiniyihch kiyâ châ-âkâ-chî iyâyuwîtâyichî awâyuwa kwâ-isinâkûhtât. Châtûhtât unikwân âku tiyâpikwâtât wâ-nikutât nâtâ â-pimûhtâyichî, nâkutât.

Âku châwât. Âku nâpât.

Âku uch utî-itipîhtâw anch iskwâuch tâpiskâyich mi-nûkun nâstîs. Kwâskupitâkinûut u Châhkâpâs, u Châhkâpâs.

"Nâsî," itikuw, "wâpâhta mâ âsinâkwâhch," itikuw. "Kâ-isinâkwâhch niya âkâ isinâkunuwâ," itikuw. Wânipiyit, âhchikâyuw wânipiyit.

"Nimisa," itâw, "ninikwân," itâw. Châschîhtâhk unikwân. "Pâsû," itâw, "nisîkusim," itâw, "kiyâ nit-âpikusîm," itâw, "kiyâ nit-anischikuchâsim," itâw. Mâyikut. Châchipâhtât châchinât.

Âukunî uyâyuwa pîsimwa tâpikwâtâw pîsimwa. Ki-wâwâyichâpiyuwânî kwâ-ihtiyichî. Mi-chî-michimâ chichinâw âspis aniyâ chisuyichî kîpwâ.

path, just when he seemed to be close to it, he would fall asleep!

The sun had already gone by the time he reached the end of the path. It had passed him by. And by the time he woke up again, it had already set off on its journey. He was never able to see it!

"What is going on here?" he asked himself.

Then he had an idea. "I'll snare it," he thought, "and then I'll be able to see it!" He set off to find his sister. "Now then, Big Sister," he said, "bring me that strand of hair there! I have a use for it," he said. And so, of course, his sister gave him the strand of hair, as he called it. That's what she gave him.

Next, he took the strand of hair and made it big and made it long. He blew on it to make it strong, so that no one could break it. He set off, taking his snare with him, to set it in the sun's path. He hung it there across the sun's path to snare it.

Now then, he went back home and went to sleep.

During the night, as the women sat together, they didn't notice anything unusual. But come the morning, they woke Chahkapas.

"Little Brother!" his sister said to him. "Look at this! Everything looks different!" she said. He got up and saw that it was dark. It was dark when he got up.

"Big Sister," he said, "my snare." He remembered his snare. "Bring me my weasel, my mouse, and my squirrel," he said. She did as he asked and gave them to him. Chahkapas set off running, running toward his snare.

And there was the sun. He had snared the sun! It seemed to be swaying from side to side. He couldn't run near it, of course—it was too hot.

Utâ wâhchi-wâpinât usîkusima. "Piskâhtâh!" itâw unikwân. Kwâ-ati-pipâtikûhkisuyichî mi-chî-piskâhtimiyuwa, nipâhikisuyuwa.

Mîn ut-anischikuchâsima iyâpich kwâ-ihtiyichî, iyâpich nipâhikisuyuwa.

Âpikusîsa an ut-âpikusîma ki-pûpûtâtâsuwâ kwâ-tuwât. Kwâ-tûtuwât wiyâpinât. Nâham tâwâpitâsiniyuwa unikwân miyâhkwâhtimiyichî kwâ-pischipiyich uyâyuw upis.

Ki-ati-wâwâyichâpiyuwânî kwâ-ihtiyichî kwâ-ati-chîhchipiyichî niyâyuwa pîsimwa kwâ-ati-sâhtâyâyich kwâ-ati-chîsikâyich.

"Âkun châ-isinâkwâhch, chiki-tipiskâw nânikutinîy âku nânikutinîy chiki-chîsikâw," itâw.

Tâkusîhk. "Nimisa, âkun châ-isinâkwâhch, châ-nipâyâhkw tâpiskâchî; chiki-tipiskâw, chiki-âhchikâw, âku châ-nipâyâhkw; âku châ-chîsikâch âku châ-unîyâhkw," itâw umisa.

Âukwâkin wâhchi-tipiskâch, inânûw, nânikutinîy pîsimwa kâ-âhchikâwâ, itâchimunânûw.

Âkutâ âskwâyâchimâkinûut, îyuw atiyûhkin, âukuw Châhkâpâs, Châhkâpâs.

So from where he was, he threw his weasel at the sun, telling it, "Bite through the line!" But the weasel shrivelled in the heat of the sun. He wasn't able to bite through the line but was burned to a crisp and died!

Next, his squirrel tried the same thing, and he too was burned to a crisp and died!

Then Chahkapas blew on his little mouse, that's what he did, he blew on him. And then he threw his mouse and he landed on the snare, attaching himself to the line with his teeth. He bit the line and it snapped.

Now the sun started to move again, swaying from side to side, and then it set off on its way, then it was bright again! Then it was daytime!

"This is how things will be," said Chahkapas. "Sometimes it will be night, and sometimes it will be day," he said.

He arrived back home. "Big Sister," he said, "this is how things will be," he told her. "When it's night, we'll sleep. When it's night, when it's dark, that's when we'll sleep. Then, when it's day, we'll get up."

And that's why, people say, there is nighttime. Sometimes, when it's dark, people tell the story of how Chahkapas snared the sun.

That is the end of the legend of Chahkapas.

Naskapi-English Glossary

Abbreviations:

=	shows an alternate spelling or word origin
dim	diminutive form
na	noun, animate
nad	noun, animate, dependent
nap	noun, animate, participle
ni	noun, inanimate
nid	noun, inanimate, dependent
p(conj.)	particle (conjunction)
p(interj.)	particle (interjection)
p(gram.)	particle (grammatical)
p(manner)	particle (manner)
p(neg.)	particle (negative)
p(number)	particle (number)
p(quant.)	particle (quantity)
p(space)	particle (space)
p(time)	particle (time)
preverb	preverb
pro(alt.)	pronoun (alternate)
pro(dem.)	pronoun (demonstrative)
pro(foc.)	pronoun (focus)
pro(interrog.)	pronoun (interrogative)
pro(pers.)	pronoun (personal)
s.o.	someone
s.t.	something
vai	verb, animate intransitive
vai+o	verb, animate intransitive with object
vii	verb, inanimate intransitive
vta	verb, transitive animate
vti	verb, transitive inanimate

Notes on the glossary:

The words listed in the glossary are, for the most part, the "dictionary-style" entries for the inflected words in the text. Because of the phonological transformations of word stems common to Algonquian grammar, often the verbs listed in the glossary appear quite different from the inflected verbs as found in the text. Here are a few examples:

On pages 70 and 100, we find *châwâyichî*, which means 'he went home.' This is from the verb **chîwâw** *vai* 'go home.' The first syllable is changed from *chî* to *châ* to indicate the verb (conjunct) order. This changed form is indicated on the first syllable of verbs in this order.

On page 74, we find *kwâ-ispis-miskûsiyichî*, which means 'how strong it (then) was.' The first syllable is the conjunct preverb *kwâ-*, meaning 'next' or 'then,' indicating a time sequence. The next two syllables are *ispis-*, a preverb meaning 'a certain amount.' This is followed by the verb stem *miskûs*, meaning 'be hard or strong.' Finally, the verb suffix *-iyichî* indicates an obviative participant. In the glossary, you will find listed the dictionary entry for this word, **miskûsîw** *vai* 'be strong, be hard,' along with the various preverbs. The glossary does not contain every word as inflected in the text, but it does include every uninflected "dictionary" entry from which each inflected word is derived.

â-	*preverb*	neutral tense (conjunct)
Âchâniskwâw	*na*	cannibal woman
âhâ	*p(interj.)*	cry of alarm
âhâhâ	*p(interj.)*	cry of alarm
âhâk	*p(interj.)*	well then
âhâkâ	*p(interj.)*	well then
âhchâpâskw	*ni*	bowshaft
âhchâpâtuy	*ni*	bowstring
âhchâpîy	*na*	bow
âhchikâw	*vii*	be dark
âhchipîhtâw	*vai*	move hand
âhchistim	*vti*	move s.t.
âhchîw	*vai*	move
âkâ	*p(conj.)*	not
âkâwiy	*p(interj.)*	don't
akiskw	*na*	arrow
akitâskw	*ni*	axe
âku	*p(interj.)*	so
akûhchin	*vai*	float
âkun	*pro(foc.)*	so this one
âkunâham	*vti*	cover s.t.
akunâw	*vta*	take s.o. off of heat / stove / fire
âkus	*p(interj.)*	in any circumstance
âkutâ	*p(interj.)*	okay
akutâw	*vai*	hang it up
âkuwâskusin	*vai*	go behind trees out of sight
akwâham	*vti*	scoop solid out of liquid in a pot
akwânâw	=	**akunâw**
akwânim	*vti*	imperative, take off the fire / stove / heat
akwâpâham	*vti*	scoop out [liquid]
amiskw	*na*	beaver
an	*pro(dem.)*	that
anch	*pro(dem.)*	those
anischikuchâs	*na*	squirrel
aniya	*pro(dem.)*	that (obv.)
aniyuwa	*pro(dem.)*	that (obv.)
antâ	*pro(dem.)*	there

âpichîhtâw	*vai+o*	use
âpîhtuwâskw	*p(space)*	halfway up a tree
âpikus	=	**âpikusîs**
âpikusîs	*na*	mouse
apis	*ni*	rope, line, string
apisâskusuw	*vai*	be small in diameter, stick-like
apisîsuw	*vai*	be small
âpitâsîhtâkinâskw	*ni*	doorpost
apuw	*vai*	sit, be laid
asâm	*na*	snowshoe
aschîhkus	*ni*	small pail
aschîhkw	*ni*	pail
aschîy	*ni*	earth, ground, land
âsi-	*preverb*	thus, in a certain way (changed form)
âsîhkwâw	*vta*	scream in pain / anger to s.o.
asimâw	*vta*	feed s.o.
asinîy	*ni*	rock
âskiyâskw	=	**ayâskw**
âskw	*p(time)*	later
astâw	*vai+o*	be placed, sit
astwâw	*vta*	save (anim) food
asuch	*p(space)*	along the shore
ati-	*preverb*	while, begin, although
âti-	*preverb*	while, begin, although (changed form)
atîhkw	*na*	caribou
atiyûhkin	*na*	legend
atuch	*p(conj.)*	not
âukun	*pro(foc.)*	it's that one
âukunî	*pro(foc.)*	that one
âukuw	*pro(foc.)*	it's that one here
âukuwîchâ	*pro(foc.)*	that's probably the one (dubitative inflection)
âukuya	=	**âukuyuw**
âukuyuw	*pro(foc.)*	it's that one here
âukuyuwa	*pro(foc.)*	it's that one here (obv.)
âukw	*pro(foc.)*	that's it

âukwâkin	*pro(foc.)*	that is the one
âukwânâ	=	**âukwâyâ**
âukwâyâ	*pro(foc.)*	there that one goes
awâ	*p(interj.)*	eh?
awâchâ	*pro(interrog.)*	who could it be?
awâchânichî	=	**awîchânichî**
awân	*pro(interrog.)*	who (singular)
awâs	*na*	child
awâsis	*na*	small child, infant
awâyuwa	*pro(dem.)*	someone (obv.)
awîchâ	*pro(foc.)*	that must be the one
awîchânichî	*pro(foc.)*	that must be them
âyâpichinâkusuw	*vai*	he looks important, he looks like he is worth something
âyâpisâskusuw	=	**âpisâskusuw**
ayâskw	*p(quant.)*	more
âyikunikâhwâw	*vta*	bury s.o. in snow
âyituw	*p(space)*	both sides
âyukunî	=	**âukunî**
châ	*p(interj.)*	dialogue affirmation
châ-	*preverb*	future tense (conjunct)
châchî-	*preverb*	in order to, for (conjunct)
châchisâpâyâw	*vii*	be morning
Châhkâpâs	*na*	proper name of legendary hero
châk	*p(time)*	finally
châkwân	*ni*	thing
châkwâyuwa	*pro(interrog.)*	what
châmutinâw	*vta*	steal (anim) from s.o.
châpî-	*preverb*	fast (changed form)
châskâ	*p(manner)*	for nothing
châstinâs	*p(interj.)*	surely
châtûutâw	=	**chîtûutâw**
chi-	*preverb, prefix*	2nd person
chî-	*preverb*	can, be able to
chî-	*preverb*	past tense (independent)
chichinâw	*vta*	take out
chîhchipâhtâw	*vai*	run off, start off
chîhchipiyuw	*vai*	start off

chîhchiwâ	*p(manner)*	really
chîhtisimâw	*vta*	run away from s.o.
chiki-	*preverb*	you will, 2nd person future tense (independent)
chikisâm	*p(manner)*	done while wearing snowshoes
chimisim	*vti*	cut s.t. short
chimisuw	*vai*	stand erect, upright, be erect
chimitâw	*vai+o*	set upright
chimiyâw	*vta*	stand it (anim) up, set it (anim) upright
chimûtimâw	*vta*	steal from s.o.
chimutuw	*vai*	steal
chinistipikâpûusuw	*vai*	stand up quickly
chinwâpâchîhtâw	*vai+o*	make long
chinwâpâchisuw	*vai*	be long, string-like
chinwâskusuw	*vai*	be long / tall, stick like
chinwâskwâhâw	*vta*	make a long stick / tree
chipâh-	*preverb*	you should, 2nd person obligatory
chipâhwâw	*vta*	close / block s.o. in
chipîchiwâhikin	*ni*	cover, lid
chipîchiwâhwâw	*vta*	put cover on it (anim)
chipiskinâhch	*p(space)*	blockage of trail
chipiskwâhch	*p(space)*	at the doorway
chîsâhâw	*vta*	finish it (anim)
chisâyâkw	*na*	bear
chîschâkâw	*vii*	be a cliff
chischâyihtim	*vti*	know s.t.
chischâyimâw	*vta*	know s.o.
chisâîyuw	*na*	elder
chischîhtim	*vti*	remember s.t.
chîschin-isuw	*vai*	dim, lie down
chischuw	*vai*	be conscious
chîsi-	*preverb*	finish
chîsikâw	*vii*	be day
chisipiyuw	*vai*	go fast
chiskuwâw	*vta*	wear it (anim) (used here for 'wearing' unborn children)

chîskwâyâpimuw	*vai*	feel dizzy
chistutâw	*vta*	reply to (cf. stutâw, kistutâw)
chistuw	*vai*	make a sound
chisuw	*vai*	be hot
chîswâyâhchîw	*vai*	move strongly
chit-	*preverb, prefix*	2nd person (before vowel)
chitâhuyâw	*vta*	take s.o. away
chîtâpimâw	*vta*	look at s.o.
chitûhtâw	*vai*	go, leave
chitustuwâw	*vai*	lay perfectly still, not move a muscle
chitutâw	*vta*	call out, reply, make noise to s.o.
chitûutânâw	*vta*	take off load from back
chîtûutâw	*vta*	carry load on back
chîwâhtâhâw	*vta*	carry s.o. home
chîwâpinâw	*vta*	throw s.o. back
chîwâpiyuw	*vai*	swim back
chîwâtisâhwâw	*vta*	send s.o. back home
chîwâtûutâw	*vai+o*	take load home on back
chîwâw	*vai*	go home, go back, return
chîwâyuwâpiyihuw	*vai*	turn self / whole body around
chîy	*pro(pers.)*	you
chîyânuw	*pro(pers.)*	we, us (inclusive)
chiyipi-	*preverb*	fast
chiyipichuw	*vai*	grow up fast
chîyipi-nîhtâuchuw	*vai*	grow up fast
ihtâw	*vai*	be present
ihtûtim	*vti*	do it
ihtûtuwâw	*vta*	do to s.o.
ihtuw	*vai*	do
inânûw	*vai*	people say
îpwâhkâw	*vai*	be smart, be alert / conscious
isâkw	*ni*	metal
ischimâw	*vai*	paddle somewhere
isi-	*preverb*	thus, in a certain way
isikâpûuw	*vai*	stand a certain way
isinâkûhtâw	*vai+o*	make look a certain way
isinâkûhuw	*vai+o*	make body look a certain way, like so

isinâkuhwâw	=	**isinâkwâhâw**
isinâkun	*vii*	look a certain way
isinâkusuw	*vai*	look so, look like, look thus
isinâkwâhâw	*vta*	make s.o. to look a certain way
isinîhkâsuw	*vai*	be named
isinîhkâtâw	*vta*	call s.o. a name, name s.o.
isinîhkâtim	*vti*	name s.t.
isinuwâw	*vta*	see as in a dream or vision
isitâsuw	*vai*	sing a song, make noise by mouth
iskâpimâw	=	**iskwâpimâw**
iskunâw	*vii*	be remaining
iskupukuyuw	*vai*	be some (food) left over
iskupwâw	*vta*	leave some (anim) uneaten
iskwâpimâw	*vta*	see for a certain distance, see s.o. for the last time
iskwâs	*na*	girl
iskwâsuw	*vai*	be burned
iskwâswâw	*vta*	burn s.o.
iskwâw	*na*	woman
îskwâw	*vii*	it ends
îskwâyâchimâw	*vta*	come to the end of a story
ispihâw	*vai*	be a certain distance
ispis	*preverb*	a certain amount, distance or time
ispisâw	*vii*	be a certain length
ispitâskusuw	*vai*	be a certain length of stick
ispitâw	*vta*	pull s.o. thus
ispitim	*vti*	move to s.t.
ispitisuw	*vai*	be a certain size
ispituw	*vai*	be a certain size
ispiyihusuw	*vai*	move whole body
ispiyuw	*vai/vii*	go, move, happen
îstikutâw	*vai+o*	be at a certain height (eg., halfway)
itâchimâw	*vta*	tell about s.o.
itâchimuw	*vai*	tell a story
itâhwâw	*vta*	wound s.o.

itâpâkiskâw	*vai+o*	lay it (string-like) so
itâpimâsuw	*vai*	look from there
itâw	*vta*	say to s.o.
itâyihtâkun	*vii*	seem like
itâyihtâkusuw	*vai*	seem like
itâyihtim	*vti*	think of / about s.t.
itâyimâw	*vta*	think of s.o.
itimutâwâw	*vta*	attach it (anim)
itipuw	*vai*	sit thus
itisimâw	*vta*	feed s.o. in such a way
itisumâw	*vta*	order s.o.
ititim	*vti*	have s.t. so
itûhtâw	*vai*	go
ituwâuw	*vai*	make vocal sounds
itwâhkâtuwâw	*vta*	yell at s.o.
iyâchistim	*vti*	struggle against s.t.
iyâhtikw	*na*	black spruce
iyâmipiyuw	*vai*	fall off
iyâpich	*p(interj.)*	nevertheless
iyaw	*vai+o*	do it
iyâw	*vta*	place, have it (anim)
iyâyâhchipitim	*vti*	move / rock s.t.
iyâyâhchipiyitâwâw	*vta*	move / rock s.o.
iyâyituw	*p(space)*	along both sides
iyâyiwâw	=	**iyâyuwâw**
iyâyuwâw	*vta*	destroy s.o.
iyâyuwîtâw	*vai+o*	break, destroy
iyimihâw	*vta*	talk to s.o.
iyimuwâw	*vai*	be a talker
iyipîhchâhâw	*vta*	keep s.o. alive
iyipîhchâw	*vai*	keep alive, heal, cure
iyûhtâpitim	*vta*	open door
îyuw	*na*	human, person
îyuw	*vai*	be alive, be born
kâ-	*preverb*	past tense (conjunct)
kâchî-	*preverb*	past tense (conjunct)
Kâchîtuwâskw	*na*	proper name of legendary foe-creature

kâkiyâ	*p(interj.)*	particle of doubt
kâpit	=	contraction of **âkâ pitimâ**
Kâwâwâpisuwâhâch	*nap*	swing people (proper name of legendary tricksters)
kâyâw	*vta*	hide s.o.
ki-	*preverb*	indirect present
kichâhchîhtuw	*vai*	do things competently
kichâmutimâw	*vta*	steal s.o.
kichîhkâhwâw	*vta*	chip / whittle branches from log / stick (anim)
kimâ	*p(interj.)*	I wish that...
kinuwâpimâw	*vta*	look after s.o., keep s.o.
kinuwâyihtim	*vti*	look after s.t., keep s.t.
kîpwâ	*p(interj.)*	indeed
kischuw	*vai*	be cooked tender
kistutâw	=	**chistutâw**
kiyâ	*p(conj.)*	and
kûhchipiyihâw	*vta*	swallow s.o.
kûn	*na*	snow
kuschâw	*vai*	fish
kuskin	*ni*	fish hook
kuskupiyuw	*vai*	wake up suddenly
kustâchimâw	*vta*	frighten s.o. by speech
kustâtâyihtâkusuw	*vai*	be ferocious, be dangerous, cause fear
kustâtikusîw	*vai*	be dangerous
kustâw	*vta*	fear s.o.
kustim	*vti*	fear s.t.
kutichiyuw	*pro(alt.)*	other (obv.)
kutik	*pro(alt.)*	other
kutinâw	*vta*	test s.o.
kutinim	*vti*	try s.t., test s.t.
kutiyâw	*vai*	swallow all the way to the end of the stomach
kutuwâw	*vai*	make a fire
kwâ-	*preverb*	next, past tense sequential (conjunct)
kwâ-chipiyihikut	=	**kûhchipiyihikut**, see **kûhchipiyihâw**

kwâstâchâ	*p(space)*	other side
mâ	*p(gram.)*	politeness discourse marker
mâh	*p(interj.)*	hark!
mâhân	*pro(dem.)*	right there, they are over there (gesture)
mâk	*p(conj.)*	so
mâkumâw	*vta*	bite s.o.
mâkupitim	*vti*	tie s.t. to
mâkwâhtim	*vti*	bite s.t.
mâmâchikunim	*vti*	hold fast to s.t.
mâmâhchikunâw	*vta*	hold fast on to s.o.
mâmâmîhkutâw	*vai+o*	carve roughly, any old way
mâmîchisuhkuwâw	*vta*	give it to eat to s.o.
mâmîhkutîhchikisuw	*na*	a red-finned fish
mân	*pro(dem.)*	over there (gesture)
mânâtâ	*pro(dem.)*	just over there (gesture)
mâniyâ	*pro(dem.)*	there, way over there (gesture)
mâniyâhkâ	*pro(dem.)*	that absent one there (gesture)
mâniyâyitâ	=	**mâniyâ**
mântâ	=	**mân + nâtâ**
mântâw	*na*	visitor, stranger
mâsâhâw	*vta*	fight with s.o.
mâskinuw	*ni*	trail, tracks, road, path
mâtisim	*vti*	cut into
mâw	*pro(dem.)*	here (gesture)
mâwâch	*p(interj.)*	no
mâwâyihtim	*vti*	take s.t. unused, just lying around, for self
mâyâyimâw	*vta*	insult, make fun of s.o.
michi-îyuw	*na*	bad person
michi-îyûw	*vai*	be a bad person
mîchim	*ni*	food
michimâ	*p(space)*	near
michisîyuw	*na*	bad person
mîchisuw	*vai*	eat
mîchiwâhp	*ni*	house, dwelling
mîchuw	*vai+o*	eat it
mîhchâpiskâw	*vii*	be a big rock

mîhchâtûch	*vai*	there are many of them
mîhchâtuw	*vai*	be many
mîhtâtâwâw	*vta*	miss s.o.
mikuskâchikuwâw	*vta*	cause trouble for s.o.
mikw	*p(conj.)*	but, only
mimâhkisâmâw	*vai*	he has / wears big snowshoes
mimâspinâw	*vai*	be really, really suffering
mimîchisuw	*vai*	eat
mimisituw	*vai*	be big (pair of)
mimiyuhkutâw	*vai+o*	carve well
mimuchîhkisuw	*vai*	heat up (may have sexual meaning)
mimûhkutâw	*vta*	carve it (anim)
mîn	*p(quant.)*	again, more, next
minâhwâw	*vta*	carry s.o. off by canoe
minâw	*vta*	take s.o. off
minîhkumuw	*vai*	strip bark
minikâhwâw	*vta*	chop down a tree to use for it
minipitâw	*vta*	pull s.o.
minisim	*vti*	cut s.t. off
misâw	*vii*	be big
misâyûkâw	*vii*	be wide, huge, broad and sheetlike
misîhtâw	*vai+o*	make big
misihwâw	*vta*	hit target (anim) with missile—arrow
misîtichisuw	*vai*	have a thick diameter
misituw	*vai*	be big
misiwâ	*p(quant.)*	all
miskim	*vti*	find s.t.
miskumîy	*na*	ice
miskûsîw	*vai*	be strong, be hard
miskûtin	*vii*	be frozen
miskuwâw	*vta*	find s.o.
miskw	*na*	bear
mistikw	*na*	tree
mistikw	*ni*	stick
mistimiskw	*na*	giant beaver
misûkuw	*vta*	hits s.o. throwing s.t.

mitisân	*na*	sweat lodge
mitisânîhkâsuw	*vai*	make a steam tent / sweat lodge for oneself
mitwâwâpisuw	*vai*	be heard swinging
mitwâsikutâhichâw	*vai*	be heard / audible breaking ice
mitwâwâskwâhichâw	*vai*	be heard / audible scraping
mîyâw	*vta*	give to s.o.
miyitâw	*p(manner)*	opposite
miyûhkutâw	*vta*	carve it (anim) nicely
miyuw	*nad*	her / his body
miywâskwâw	*vii*	be a good / nice tree
miywâw	*vii*	be good / nice
mmm	*p(interj.)*	hesitation marker
mûchihâw	*vta*	cause amusement to s.o.
mûhkutâkin	*ni*	crooked knife
mûhkutâw	*vta*	carve (anim) with a crooked knife
mumiskwâw	*vta*	eat beaver
mûsâskupâhtâsuw	*vai*	run on ice (dim)
musâskupâhtâw	*vai*	run on ice
musâwâw	*vai*	go into water
muschîhkûnichinâw	*vta*	pull s.o. out of snow
mûsinâw	*p(time)*	always
muskâmuskâchûsuw	*vai*	bob up and down while being boiled
mustinim	*vti*	take hold of s.t.
muwâw	*vta*	eat it (anim)
muyâm	*p(manner)*	just like, exactly the same, serves her / him right
mwâmiskwâw	=	**mumiskwâw**
nâ	*pro(dem)*	that over there
nâââ	*p(interj.)*	look at him
nâch	*pro(dem)*	those over there
nâham	*p(manner)*	properly, orderly
nâhâw	*p(manner)*	exactly right
nama	*p(neg.)*	not, no; also rendered as a contraction, **mi-**
namayâw	*pro(dem.)*	not him / her / it; also **miyâw**

nânâkichâhâw	*vta*	watch s.o.
nânâmipiyuw	*vai/vii*	tremble
nânâskânâw	*vta*	pull s.o. hand over hand
nânikutinîy	*p(time)*	sometimes
nânitûnichâhâw	*vta*	try to meet (reduplication of **nitûnichâhâw**)
nânituwâpimâw	*vta*	go to hunt for / see s.o.
nânituwâpuw	*vai*	go look at
nânûchîhkim	*vti*	do s.t. to bother, deal with, fool around with s.t.
nâpâchikiskw	*na*	man (old word)
nâpâw	*na*	man
nâsch	*p(interj.)*	really
nâsî	*na*	little brother (vocative)
nâsipâtâhâw	*vta*	take s.o. down to the shore
nâsipâw	*vai*	go down to the shore, go down to Sept-Îles
nâstîs	*p(manner)*	entirely
nâstwâyihtim	*vti*	be overwhelmed by / die from s.t. (strong negative emotion, i.e., grief, anger, fear)
nâtâ	*pro(dem.)*	over there
nâtâham	*vti*	swim to s.t.
nâtâhwâw	*vta*	swim to s.o.
nâtâtuwâmutuwâw	*vta*	climb up to get s.o.
nâtâw	*vta*	go to, go towards s.o.
nâtim	*vti*	go to s.t.
nâutâ	*pro(dem.)*	there, right here (gesture)
nâyâ	*pro(dem.)*	over there
neg + unâyimâsuw	*vai*	be not in doubt
ni-	*preverb, prefix*	1st person
nichî-	*preverb*	I did, 1st person past tense (independent)
nîh	*p(manner)*	usually
nîhî	*p(interj.)*	yes
nîhtâ-	*preverb*	never
nîhtâuchuw	*vai*	grow up
nîhtâwâw	*vai*	be good at talking

niki-	*preverb*	I will, 1st person future tense (independent)
nikimuw	*vai*	sing
nikisâkâham	*vti*	break a piece off s.t.
nikitâw	*vta*	leave s.o. behind
nikutâw	*vta*	snare it (anim)
nikwân	*na*	snare
nimâs	*na*	fish
nimis	*na*	my older sister
nimisa	*na*	my older sister (vocative)
ninâhituwâw	*vta*	obey s.o.
ninâutinim	*vti*	catch s.t.
nipâh-	*preverb*	I should, 1st person obligatory
nipâhâw	*vta*	kill s.o.
nipâhîkisuw	*vai*	be burned to death
nipâw	*vai*	sleep
nîpin	*vii*	be summer
nipîy	*ni*	water
nîpûuw	*vai*	stand
nipuw	*vai*	die
nisîm	*nad*	my younger sibling
nîsinîw	*vai*	be two
nîsîyuw	*na*	future generations, descendants
niskumâw	*vta*	agree with s.o.
nîst	*pro(pers.)*	me too, you too
nîstim	*p(manner)*	first
nistûnuwâw	*vta*	recognize s.o.
nistûuch	*vai*	be three
nistwâskwâhâw	*vta*	make three (anim) sticks
nistwâw	*p(quant.)*	three times
nîsûch	*vai*	be two
nîswâpîhkâtim	*vti*	tie two together
nîswâpikâtâw	*vta*	tie two (anim) together
nit-	*preverb, prefix*	1st person (before vowel)
nitâsimich	*na*	my conjuring tools
nitimikw	*p(space)*	anywhere
nitûhtuwâw	*vta*	hear s.o., listen to
nitûnichâhâw	*vta*	try to meet s.o.

nituwâpâhtim	*vti*	go to see s.t.
nituwâpimâw	*vta*	go to see s.o.
nituwâyimâw	*vta*	want / need s.o.
nituwîsuw	*vai*	feed selves from
nitwâkiminâw	*vta*	search in water by hand, feel around for s.o.
nitwâkiminichâw	*vai*	search in water by hand, feel around
nîy	*pro(pers.)*	me, I
niya	*pro(dem.)*	that
niyâhkâ	*pro(dem.)*	that absent one
niyâyuw	*pro(dem.)*	those
niyâyuwa	*pro(dem.)*	those (obv.)
nûchihäw	*vta*	bother s.o.
nuchîhkim	*vti*	be busy with, deal with s.t.
nûchîhkuwâw	*vta*	deal with, be busy with, be occupied with s.o.
nûhtâpuwâsiw	*vta*	stir (anim) liquid
nûhtâwîy	*nad*	my father
nûkun	*vii*	be visible
nutîhtâhwâw	*vta*	come upon s.o. by canoe
nûtimâskusuw	*vai*	be a whole stick / tree
nûtimikûhchipiyihâw	*vta*	swallow s.o. whole
nûtinâw	*vta*	catch it (anim) with hand
nûtinimiskwâhâw	*vta*	go get beaver
pâchî-	*preverb*	toward speaker
pâchîhtâw	*vai+o*	let go of it, let it fall, drop it
pâchinuwâkâpiskâw	*vii*	be rock slanted in this direction
pâchisin	*vai*	fall, drop
pâchi-tikusin	*vai*	arrive here
pâhkunâw	*vta*	skin an animal
pâhpuw	*vai*	laugh
pâhtuwâw	*vta*	hear s.o.
pâikw	*p(number)*	one
pâkistuwâpitâw	*vta*	pull s.o. under water
pâkupiyuw	*vai*	wake up
pânîhchuwâskim	*vti*	move / force s.t. open with foot or body
pâpâhtâkusuhuw	*vai*	be heard without being seen

pâpîhtâham	*vti*	put into s.t.
pâpîkuswâw	*vta*	cut (anim) in pieces
pâschin	=	**pâchisin**
pâstinâw	*vta*	put (anim) down, drop
pâsunâkusuw	*vai*	appear to be near
pâsuwâw	*vta*	bring s.o.
pâtâw	*vai+o*	bring
pâtûhtâw	*vai*	come this way
pâtûtâw	*vta*	walk towards s.o.
pâtus	*p(time)*	later
pâtwâtim	*vti*	heard singing while coming this direction
pîhchâw	*vai*	enter
pîhtâhwâw	*vta*	put s.o. in
pîhtâtusâhwâw	*vta*	send s.o. in
pîhtâyâkunichipiyihuw	*vai*	dive into snow with whole body
pîhtâyâskunimuwâw	*vta*	poke a stick in at s.o.
pîhtikâhâw	*vta*	bring / take s.o. in
pîhtikimîhch	*p(space)*	inside
pîhtikitâw	*vai*	bring inside
pîhtikuwâw	*vta*	go inside s.o.'s place / house
pîhtûhtâw	*vai*	come / enter walking, walk in this direction
pikistuwâhwâw	*vta*	put (anim) in water
pîkunim	*vti*	break s.t. by hand (take off the covering)
pîkupitâw	*vta*	tear (anim) open / apart, break by tearing
pîkupitim	*vti*	tear down, break by tearing / pulling
pîkusûkunâhwâu	*vta*	break someone's hip by instrument
pîkuswâw	*vta*	cut off, break (anim) by cutting
pikwâham	*vti*	damage s.t.
pikwâhichâw	*vai*	chop hole in ice
pikwâtâuw	*vai*	wear as a belt
pimâhâw	*vta*	take s.o. by canoe / paddling
pîmâhkuyâpitâw	*vta*	twist (anim) back on itself

pimâskusin	*vai*	lie along, straight
pimâyimâw	*vta*	bother s.o.
pimîchikistâw	*vai*	be fat, e.g., have fat over ribs, man or animal
pimipâhtâsuw	*vai*	run (dim)
pimipâhtâw	*vai*	run
pimipâyituw	*vta*	run with / carrying s.o.
pimisin	*vai*	lie down, be lying down
pimiskâw	*vai*	paddle swim
pimiskupâhtâw	*vai*	run on ice
pimîsuw	*vai*	be greasy
pimîy	*ni*	fat, grease
pimuchâw	*vai*	throw, shoot an arrow
pimûhtâw	*vai*	walk, travel
pimutim	*vti*	let fly a missile at s.t.
pimwâw	*vta*	shoot s.o., let fly at s.o.
pipâhtâwâyimusuw	*vta*	be heard
pipâmâkuyâpitâw	*vta*	keep twisting (anim) back on itself
pipâmatâchimipâhtâw	*vai*	crawl around
pipâmûhtâw	*vai*	walk around
pipâsichinim	*vta*	break s.o.'s hand
pipâsikwâpinâpitâw	*vta*	break s.o.'s hand / wrist
pipâtikukisuw	*vai*	shrivel in heat
pipichikâhwâw	*vta*	chop (anim. tree) in thin strips
pipîhpimuwâw	*vta*	throw at s.o.
pipikâhâw	*vta*	cook s.o. by boiling
pipîmâhkunâpitâw	=	**pipâmâkuyâpitâw**
pisâpâchîwâsuw	*vai*	be skinny
pischipiyuw	*vai/vii*	snap / break cord, thread, rope
pisikusipâhtâw	*vai*	stand up quickly
pisikuw	*vai*	get up
pisim	*vti*	cut s.t. (string-like)
pîsim	*na*	sun
pîsîtikâhwâw	*vta*	break (anim) into pieces
piskâpâsim	*vti*	relational, cut s.t. (string-like)
piskâpâsuw	*vai*	cut (string-like)
piskâtim	*vai+o*	break it (string-like)

piskiswâw	*vta*	cut open (anim) gut
piskutinâw	*vii*	be a mountain
piskwâhichâw	*vai*	scrape hides
pispinâ	*p(manner)*	particle of doubt
pistinâw	*vta*	drop, let go of s.o.
pistûutâw	*vta*	unload s.o. from back
pîtikimîhch	*p(space)*	inside
pitimâ	*p(time)*	right away
piyâchi-	*preverb*	toward speaker (changed form)
pûpûtâhtim	*vti*	blow on s.t. repeatedly
pûpûtâtâw	*vta*	blow on s.o. repeatedly
pûstûutâw	*vta*	put s.o. on back (to carry)
putâkimipiyuw	*vai*	fall into water / liquid
pûtâtâw	*vta*	blow on s.o.
sâchiskwâsimâw	*vta*	make s.o.'s head stick out
sâchiskwâsin	*vta*	lie with head sticking out
sâchiwâpimâw	*vta*	looks over at s.o. / it (anim)
sâchiwâpiyuw	*vai*	peek out at s.o.
sâkâpitâw	*vta*	tie s.o. to a line
sâkâskwâw	*vai*	come out of woods
sâkichuwâw	*vai*	climb
sâkwâhâw	*vta*	overcome s.o.
sâkwâskâham	*vti*	walk out of the trees
sâkwâskusuw	*vai*	be thin / narrow trees
sâkwâskwâham	*vai*	come out of the woods / thin trees
sâpisuw	*vai*	be strong
sâpiyuw	*vai*	back off, step back
sâpuchin	*vai*	be pierced
sâpwâskusimâw	*vta*	pierce s.o.
sâs	*p(time)*	already
sâskwâsimâw	=	**sâchiskwâsimâw**
sichinâw	*vta*	hold by the handle
sîhtâyâw	*vii*	be bright light
sikâpitim	*vti*	tie s.t. on to s.t.
sîkus	*na*	weasel
siniakusuw	*vai*	look thus
siskâhupâhtâsuw	*vai+o*	run with a stick / cane / bow
sistikw	*ni*	strand of hair

sisuwîkwâkunikâw	*vii*	be blood-stained snow
sîtutîhkwâmâ+suw	*vta*	carry s.o. under arm
sîtwâyimâw	*vta*	keep s.o. company
stûhtâw	=	**chitûhtâw**
stutâw	=	**chistutâw**
sûhchâyihtâkusuw	*vai*	seem to be strong, capable of hard work
sûhkâpâkin	*vii*	be strong (string-like)
sûnâskwâtâham	*vti*	skate on s.t.
sûnimâw	*vta*	capable of bending it (anim, bow)
sûnisûnâskwâtâsuw	*vai*	skate around
sûsûwîhkutâw	*vta*	sand, carve smooth (anim, wood)
tâhkûhch	*p(space)*	on top of a surface
tâhkunâw	*vta*	hold s.o.
tâhkunim	*vti*	hold s.t.
tâmîhch	*p(space)*	underneath
tân	*pro(interrog.)*	how
tântâ	*pro(interrog.)*	where
tâpâ	*p(conj.)*	no, not
tâpâkâ	*p(time)*	since obviously
tâpikwâtâw	*vta*	snare it (anim), lasso, put a string around
tâpikwâw	*vai+o*	set a snare
tâpititûw	*vai*	be together
tâpwâ	*p(manner)*	really, truly
tâw	=	**ihtâw**
tâwâpitâsin	*vai*	land in the middle after being thrown
tikun	*vii*	be present
tikusîhtâhâw	*vta*	arrive bringing s.o.
tikusin	*vai*	arrive
tikusûhûtâw	*vai*	arrive with load on back
tipâhamâsuw	*vai*	take / seek revenge
tipâhamuwâw	*vta*	avenge s.o.
tipâmâsuw	=	**tipâhamâsuw**
tipiskâw	*vii*	be night
tistuwâhîkin	*ni*	crossed poles at the top of a teepee

titâpwâtuwâw	*vta*	tell the truth to, comply with s.o. (do as told)
tûmîhkwâna	*ni*	fat container
tûtim	=	**ihtûtim**
tûtuwâw	=	**ihtûtuwâw**
tuw	=	**ihtuw**
twâmuwâw	*vta*	point at s.o.
u	*pro(dem.)*	this
u-	*preverb, prefix*	3rd person
uch	*pro(dem.)*	these
uchipichitim	*vti*	grab s.t.
uchipitâw	*vta*	pull s.o. from there
uchipitim	*vti*	pull s.t.
ûhch	=	**ûhchi**
ûhchi-	*preverb*	source
uhchikâpitim	*vti*	tie to s.t. from there
ûhchi-sâpimâw	*vta*	pierce s.o.
ûhchi-sâpuchin	*vai*	be pierced from there
ûhchi-tâhkunâw	*vta*	hold on tightly
ûhpitâw	*vta*	lift s.o.
ûhtâpâkimuw	*vii*	it (string-like) comes from there
ûhtâwîw	*vai*	have a father
ûhtâwîya	*nad*	her / his father
ukâwîw	*vai*	have a mother
ukâwîya	*nad*	her / his mother
ukiskukâsuw	*vai*	make arrow(s) for self
ukiskutuwâw	*vta*	use (anim) for / as an arrow
umisa	*nad*	her / his older sister
unâpâm	*nad*	her husband
unâpâmisuwâwa	*nad*	their husband (from **unâpâm**)
unâyihtim	*vti*	be vague about s.t., be unaware of s.t.
unâyimâw	*vta*	be unaware of s.o.
unînâw	*vta*	wake s.o. up, rouse s.o.
unipâkinîhkuwâw	*vta*	make a blanket for s.o.
unîpiyuw	*vai*	get up from prone position
unîw	*vai*	get up
upischunâmâw	*vta*	lift s.o. with trunk

upîwiy	*ni*	hair
upiywâwîw	*vii*	be hairy
usâ	=	**wâsâ**
usâm	*p(quant.)*	many
uschâchikunâw	*vii*	stick out of snow
uschinîchisuw	*na*	young man
uschîsikw	*nid*	eye
uschûn	*nad*	its trunk
uschuy	*nad*	fish stomach
usîhtâw	*vai+o*	make it
usîma	*nad*	her / his younger sibling
usimiskwâw	*vta*	boil beaver
usinâw	=	**usinuwâw**
usinuwâw	*vta*	laugh at s.o.
uskuy	*na*	birch tree
uspiskun	*nid*	her / his back
ustâhkunâw	*vta*	hold fast to, hold on to s.o.
ustikwân	*nid*	head
ustikwânikâm	*vti*	shape the end of s.t. into a head
ustin	*ni*	nest
ustipâch	*p(space)*	on top of
usûkin	*nid*	lower back, tailbone, rear end
ususinuwâw	*vta*	repeatedly laugh at s.o.
usuy	*nid*	tail
ut-	*preverb, prefix*	3rd person (before vowel)
utâ	*p(space)*	here
utâchistuwâw	*vta*	pull string on (anim) bow
utâhch	*p(space, time)*	in back, at the rear; in the past
utâhchâpâtuw	*vai*	put string on bow
utâhwâw	*vta*	inhale s.o. using an instrument
utâkusîw	*vii*	be evening
utâmistikwânâhwâw	*vta*	hit s.o. on head
utânisa	*nad*	her / his daughter
utâpitâsîhtânuw	*vii*	be used as a doorpost
utâsima	*na*	her / his conjuring tools
utâtim	*vti*	take in mouth, inhale, suck in s.t.
ut-awâsîmîhkuwâw	*vta*	be made pregnant
utî-	*preverb*	while

utîhchinim	*vti*	reach s.t. by hand
utîhchipitâw	*vta*	reach s.o.
utîhchîy	*nid*	her / his hand
utîhkutimisa	*nad*	his nephews (old word)
utîhkwiy	*nid*	armpit
utîhtâw	*vai+o*	reach to
utîhtim	*vti*	come upon s.t.
utinâw	*vta*	take s.o.
utinim	*vti*	take s.t.
utinimiskwâhâw	*vta*	make s.o. go after beaver
utinimiskwâw	*vai*	go after beaver
utischitân	*nid*	her / his lower leg
utitâmâham	*vti*	hit s.t.
utitâmâhâw	=	**utitâmâhwâw**
utitâmâhwâw	*vta*	hit s.o. repeatedly
utitâmischitâunâhwâw	*vta*	hit on calf repeatedly
utitâmîstâhwâw	*vta*	hit on feet repeatedly
utitâmistikwânâhwâw	*vta*	hit on head repeatedly
utiy	=	**uschuy**
utûn	*nid*	mouth
ut-ûwtuw	*vai*	have a canoe
uwa	*pro(dem.)*	this (obv.)
uwâtinâw	*vta*	grab s.o.
ûwt	*ni*	boat, canoe
uya	*pro(dem.)*	this (obv.)
uyâhch	*pro(dem.)*	in her body
uyâyîhch	*pro(dem.)*	on their bodies (from **miyuw**)
uyâyuw	*pro(dem.)*	this one
uyâyuwa	*pro(dem.)*	those ones (obv.)
wâ-	*preverb*	want, volition (changed form)
wâchinâkinâhtikw	*na*	tamarack tree
wâhchi-	*preverb*	source (changed form)
wâhyuwîs	*p(space)*	not far
wâpâhtim	*vti*	see s.t.
wâpimâw	*vta*	see s.o.
wâpin	*vii*	be dawn
wâpinâw	*vta*	throw (anim) away
wâpinikuschâw	*vai*	set hook in water overnight

wâpiskuwâw	*vta*	flick / fling (anim) away (by foot or body)
wâpiskw	*na*	polar bear
wâs	*p(conj.)*	for
wâsâ	*p(interj.)*	really
wâsâ usâm	=	**wâsâm**
wâsâm	*p(interj.)*	too much, too far (expression of exclamation)
wâskâpistuwâw	*vta*	sit in a circle around s.o.
wâtâspisuw	*vai*	get dressed
wâukimâw	*vta*	swallow s.o. whole
wâuswâpâkâmuwâw	*vta*	splash s.o. with it
wâwâch	*p(manner)*	evidently
wâwâpîhchânâw	*vta*	make s.o. swing
wâwâpisuhâw	*vta*	swing s.o.
wâwâpisunâw	*vta*	swing s.o.
wâwâpisuw	*vai*	swings
wâwâtâspisuw	*vai*	get dressed
wâwâtâyihtim	*vti*	plan s.t.
wâwâtîhkutâw	*vta*	carve (anim) carefully
wâwâtipuw	*vai*	sit comfortably
wâwâyichâpiyuw	=	**wâwâyichipiyuw**
wâwâyichipiyuw	*vai/vii*	sway, move from side to side
wâyuwîs	*p(space)*	a little ways off, not as far
wî-	*preverb*	want, volition
wîch	*nid*	home, dwelling
wîchâwâkin	*na*	friend, companion
wîchâwâw	*vta*	go with s.o.
wîchikâpûstuwâw	*vta*	stand with s.o.
wîchiwâw	*ni*	their place
wîchuw	*vai*	live
wîhchâkitiyâmâw	*vta*	cause s.o. to smell bad
wîhkiyâsâw	*vta*	trick s.o.
wîhkwâsâkâw	*vii*	be stone
wîhkwâsuw	*vai*	be round-ended, be bag-like
wîhtimuwâw	*vta*	tell s.o.
wîhtûkiy	*nid*	ear
wîmâskuwâw	*vta*	pass s.o. by

wîpich	*p(time)*	soon
wîskichân	*na*	grey jay
wîst	*ni*	beaver lodge
wîtihâw	*vta*	take s.o. outside
wîtimipimâw	*vta*	sit with s.o.
wîwa	*nad*	his wife
wîwîpiyihuw	*vai*	whole body goes out
wîwîtihâw	*vta*	take s.o. outside
wîwîtimîhch	*p(space)*	outside
wîwîtisinâw	*vta*	take outside by hand, throw outside
wîwîw	*vai*	go out
wîy	*pro(pers.)*	she / he, him / her
wîyâpiniyich	*vii*	be the following day
wiyâsihtûtuwâw	*vta*	do s.t. strange to s.o., conjure for s.o.
wiyâyuw	*pro(dem.)*	that there
wiyâyuwa	*pro(dem.)*	that there (obv)
yâyâhchîsuw	*vai*	move around

Other books in the
First Nations Language Readers series:

wawiyatācimowinisa /
ᐊᐧᐃᐧᔭᑖᒋᒧᐃᐧᓂᓴ /
Funny Little Stories
narrated by Cree-speaking students,
instructors, and Elders;
edited by Arok Wolvengrey

Nēnapohš āhtahsōkēwinan /
ᓀᓇᐳᐦᐡ ᐋᐦᑕᐦᓲᑫᐃᐧᓇᐣ /
Nēnapohš Legends
narrated by Saulteaux Elders;
transcribed, translated and edited
by Margaret Cote

Ákaitsinikssiistsi /
Blackfoot Stories of Old
written, translated, and edited by
Ikkináínihki *Lena Heavy Shields Russell*
and Piitáákii *Inge Genee*

nīhithaw ācimowina /
ᓃᐦᐃᖬᐤ ᐋᒋᒧᐃᐧᓇ /
Woods Cree Stories
written and translated by
Solomon Ratt

Nilh Izá Sptákwlhkalh /
niɬ ʔizá sptákʷɬkaɬ /
These Are Our Legends
narrated by Lillooet Elders;
transcribed and translated by Jan van Eijk

ʔɔʔɔɔɔniiih wɔɔchʔɔɔɔnɔh /
Aaniiih / Gros Ventre Stories
Told by Aaniiih / Gros Ventre Elders
and/or retold by Terry Brockie
Edited and Translated by Terry Brockie
and Andrew Cowell

www.ingramcontent.com/pod-product-compliance
Lightning Source LLC
Chambersburg PA
CBHW031558060326
40783CB00026B/4137
* 9 7 8 0 8 8 9 7 7 8 2 9 0 *